RENÉ LÉVESQUE

An Option
for Quebec

McClelland and Stewart

Originally published in French, 1968, by
Les Éditions de L'Homme, Montréal.

0-7710-5290-1

The Canadian Publishers
McClelland and Stewart Limited
25 Hollinger Road, Toronto

PRINTED IN CANADA

By Way of a Foreword: The Moment of Choice 7

Preface 9

Part One: A Country That Must Be Made 13

Chapter **1** "Belonging" 14

Chapter **2** The Acceleration of History 15

Chapter **3** The Quiet Revolution 18

Chapter **4** The Basic Minimums 20

Chapter **5** The Blind Alley 24

Chapter **6** The Way of the Future 27

Part Two: A Country That Is "Feasible" 31

Chapter **1** The Association 35

Chapter **2** The Transition Period 47

Part Three: Appendices 57

Appendix **1** Some Varieties of Special Status 58

Appendix **2** Neo-Centralization 66

Appendix **3** Quebec–Canada: A Blind Alley 71

Appendix **4** The Snare of Biculturalism 82

Appendix **5** Association of Sovereign States 94

Appendix **6** Other Testimony 108

Appendix **7** Operation Panic 119

Conclusion 122

Epilogue 126

By Way of a Foreword: The Moment of Choice

You are not quite a social being worthy of the term unless you have a fatherland which is your own and incontestably so. In most cases we are born into the fatherland; but alas! it also often happens that we have to reconquer it.

Jacques Madaule

Last October we left the Liberal Party of Quebec.

Six months earlier some twenty of us had met at an inn at Mont Tremblant to find out among ourselves where we stood on the constitutional question. Against the background of numerous incidents which have been reported in the press and which we have no need to analyze here, we continued our research and the reflection which would lead us to choose a solution capable of reconciling the reality of interdependence with those exigencies of political sovereignty essential to the development of modern nations, in which the state plays such a large role in the economic, social, and cultural life of the people.

This option for a sovereign Quebec, which would be associated with the rest of Canada in a new union, is the subject of the texts we have collected in this little book, designed for all those who are concerned today about the future of Quebec and Canada.

It is not an election platform. You will not find all the answers in it. But you will find an attitude and alternative.

We have, we believe, arrived at a moment of choice.

It is an unavoidable choice which we must have the courage to consider without straying into useless quarrels over words, formulas, or personalities.

The Canadian constitutional crisis is not an "invention." It not only exists, it is growing more and more acute; it is nearing the boiling point.

Those who are disturbed by it, even those who are afraid of it, should remember that Quebec itself has brought on this crisis, and that it is therefore Quebec's responsibility to find within itself the clear thinking and the courage to bring it to its conclusion.

What is at stake? The right to live one's life, to live *our* life; the right of men to live, whether they are weak or powerful; the right of peoples and nations to live, whether they are large or small.

Like Fernand Dumont, Director of the Institute of Social Sciences at Laval University, we believe "in the quality of little nations." And, for our own, we demand the right of existence.

The life we want to live is that of free men, and we are ready to assume all the responsibilities that implies; only a child has the right to surrender those responsibilities or exchange them for any kind of tutelage, however comfortable it might be.

But nothing prevents us from wanting to live this life fully and associate freely with the lives of others—other men, other peoples—as equal partners.

That is what we are proposing to Canadians.

We see this as the only solution; not, however, in the spirit of a hopeless cause, but in the cause of hope itself!

This hope of ours is based on the conviction that free peoples and free men can unite to build a new society that will answer their needs to build the "open city" of tomorrow.

We have a country to create, and very little time in which to do it.

> *Roch Banville*
> *Rosaire Beaulé*
> *Gérard Bélanger*
> *Jean R. Boivin*
> *Marc Brière*
> *Pothier Ferland*
> *Maurice Jobin*
> *René Lévesque*
> *Monique Marchand*
> *Guy Pelletier*
> *Réginald Savoie*

Preface

From this moment on, regardless of the discords among political parties, regardless of the often only half-concealed interests of certain classes of society, regardless of the deep, emotional fear of risk, it appears indisputable that Quebec is heading down a one-way street to sovereignty.

This is not a revolutionary phenomenon. A close analysis of history shows it to be the result—which we now must refine to perfection—of a slow and laborious process that began two centuries ago. The new element is in the acceleration of the process and the increasingly acute awareness it has created in every section of Quebec's population. One feels, holding one's breath, that the climax is approaching.

Looking back now, it seems clear that the Duplessis regime contained the seeds of birth of two trends which might appear to be contradictory. The first, in reaction against years of inertia, was an attempt to promote social progress in every area of Quebec life; the second placed its emphasis on our political status and on the constitutional framework within which Quebec's destiny was to develop.

At first the contradiction between the two may have seemed irreconcilable to some. Social reformers particularly, who saw in Quebec nationalism only an artificial outlet for energies that could better have been employed in other ways—which was often the case—disagreed sharply with those who advocated a new or reformed constitution, and especially with the extremists who then were beginning to make their brutal bid for independent status.

What has been termed the *déblocage* of the sixties, *i.e.*, the progress of Quebec at a more normal rate toward the ideals familiar to every modern society, clearly showed that the contradiction between social and national progress was more imagined than real. The majority of social reformers from 1950 to 1960 were implacable enemies of the Duplessis regime and untiring critics of nationalism. The same people today find themselves hoping that the Canadian constitution will be amended to allow greater freedom of action for *la communauté nationale* of Quebec. Of little importance are the last recalcitrants who, under the sign of the dove, attempt to maintain a crumbling political *status quo*. At least they are as useful as milestones to give us a better idea of the progress we have made.

Inevitably, the social development of Quebec is related to the development of the Quebec nation to the point of being indistinguishable from it. As they grow more free, more democratic, better educated, and richer, *Québécois* necessarily are more clearly conscious of their identity as a group, and have a better understanding of sovereignty as the essential condition for improving their collective life. Social progress nourishes nationalism, until nationalism appears as the indispensable key to social progress.

And this is more or less where we stand psychologically at the moment. As to tactics, we are in search of alternatives which will either accelerate or slow down the process.

Right from the beginning, we must immediately eliminate the thesis of a better-understood, better-applied, better-respected *status quo*, as well as that of a slightly amended constitution which would have the advantage of giving equality to the two nations across the whole of Canada. The first thesis has in the last hundred years given rise to an impressive number of nationalist aberrations whose ultimate sterility is now self-evident. The second is based on that human frailty which fabricates great dreams. To understand its unrealistic character, we need only imagine how many centuries it would take before the *Québécois* from Lac St-Jean would feel really at home in the Fraser Valley.

Special status, with its many variations and its indeterminate content, has a real power of attraction at the moment. In one of its aspects it promotes a little progress, and in another a dose of caution. Thus one has the impression of moving forward in an atmosphere of security. In reality, the negative aspect is the dominant one. The thesis of a special status, as we already have said, is an expression of fear in the face of the inevitable. It is the involuntary hesitation before the final choice. It is the fear of being unable to depend on the rear-guard, the fear of seeing one's retreat cut off: as if Quebec's sovereignty meant anything more than a simple political re-arrangement in a marginal area of North America. Such a thesis, inspired by a refusal of reality, by a rejection of a calculated and thought-out risk, is bound to remain sterile or engender a monster. It was a long time before anyone took the risk of specifying any real content under the label of "special status." But the moment it was done, the absurdity of this alternative became apparent: apart from the fact that the Canadian federation was to have inflicted upon it a constitutional deformity that would make it an object of curiosity in the world–a fact that we already knew from the very enunciation of the thesis–the "privileges" accorded to Quebec, which are not a fraction of those offered by sovereignty, would give rise to just as vehement protests in other provinces as independence itself. And in this case the protests would be highly justified, for we would be asking the rest of Canada to assume the burden of a slice of autonomy that was beneficial only to ourselves.

The awkward contortions of the supporters of this thesis are useful at least inasmuch as they show Quebec's irresistible leaning toward sovereignty.

But this sovereignty is not an end in itself. It is the inevitable path along which the future of Quebec is to be found.

This is perhaps what distinguishes the Lévesque option from those of the other independence parties that have been in existence for some years. As is often the case in the history of political groups in the Western World, the RIN and the RN have had the thankless but necessary task of acting as agents to ferment ideas which most people, consciously or not, still refused to consider seriously. The propaganda that these parties had to put out in order to break down public resistance was bound to give independence the status of a final goal, a kind of absolute; this idea must obviously be rejected. But whatever they do, these parties are marked with an apolitical label. They are thought–and perhaps always will be thought–to be doctrinaire and prejudiced. They were a useful and necessary stage that had to be gone through.

The Lévesque option is the only thesis in favour of a sovereign Quebec which the latter's most determined opponents would hesitate to call a mere intellectual game. This is because, both through the man and through the broad intent of its programme, it is quite representative of that growing together of the social concern and nationalist feeling that is the most important phenomenon of recent years in Quebec. It is not only a constitutional option, it also is political. While it states the prerequisites for the development of Quebec society, it does not neglect the political and economic lines of power on the North American continent.

It is at present the most valid working hypothesis we have,

because it conforms best to the conditions of the moment, which consist on the one hand of irrepressible and ever-growing aspirations and, on the other, of a frantic search for an appropriate framework in which they can be realized.

It is this balance, achieved in line with the needs of a modern Quebec, that perhaps will make it one of the most important rallying-points in our history.

Jean Blain

A Country that Must be Made

Vive le Québec Libre!
Charles de Gaulle

For my part I believe in the
quality of small nations:
here is where common values
have a chance to sink deep roots.
Fernand Dumont

Chapter 1 "Belonging"

We are *Québécois*.

What that means first and foremost—and if need be, all that it means—is that we are attached to this one corner of the earth where we can be completely ourselves: this Quebec, the only place where we have the unmistakable feeling that "here we can be really at home."

Being ourselves is essentially a matter of keeping and developing a personality that has survived for three and a half centuries.

At the core of this personality is the fact that we speak French. Everything else depends on this one essential element and follows from it or leads us infallibly back to it.

In our history, America began with a French look, briefly but gloriously given it by Champlain, Joliet, La Salle, La-Verendrye. . . . We learn our first lessons in progress and perseverance from Maisonneuve, Jeanne Mance, Jean Talon; and in daring or heroism from Lambert Closse, Brébeuf, Frontenac, d'Iberville. . . .

Then came the conquest. We were a conquered people, our hearts set on surviving in some small way on a continent that had become Anglo-Saxon.

Somehow or other, through countless changes and a variety of regimes, despite difficulties without number (our lack of awareness and even our ignorance serving all too often as our best protection), we succeeded.

Here again, when we recall the major historical landmarks, we come upon a profusion of names: Etienne Parent and Lafontaine and the Patriots of '37; Louis Riel and Honoré Mercier, Bourassa, Philippe Hamel; Garneau and Edouard Montpetit and Asselin and Lionel Groulx. . . . For each of them, the main driving force behind every action was the will to continue, and the tenacious hope that they could make it worth while.

Until recently in this difficult process of survival we enjoyed the protection of a certain degree of isolation. We lived a relatively sheltered life in a rural society in which a great measure of unanimity reigned, and in which poverty set its limits on change and aspiration alike.

opportunity. All along the way there have been hesitations and, God knows, these still exist. In all these accomplishments mistakes have been made and gaps have been left—and whatever happens, even if we do a hundred times as much, this always will be so.

No One Will Do It For You

But in the process we have learned certain things, things which are both simple and revolutionary.

The first is that we have the capacity to do the job ourselves, and the more we take charge and accept our responsibilities, the more efficient we find we are; capable, all things considered, of succeeding just as well as anyone else.

Another is that there is no valid *excuse*, that it is up to us to find and apply to our problems the solutions that are right for us; for no one else can, much less wants to, solve them for us.

Yet another thing we have learned—and perhaps the most important: "The appetite comes with the eating." This is a phenomenon we can see everywhere as soon as a human group decides to move forward. It is called the "revolution of rising expectations."

This is the main driving force at our disposal for continued progress. We must calculate its use as precisely as possible, to avoid costly diversions; but even more we must take care not to stifle it, for without this we shall experience the collective catastrophe of an immobilized society, at a time when those who fail to advance automatically retreat, and to a point which can easily become one of no return.

In other words, above all we must guard against loss of impetus, against the periodic desire to slow down, against the belief that we are moving too quickly when in reality—despite a few wanderings—we are just beginning to reach the speed our age demands. In this, a nation is like an individual: those who succeed are those who are unafraid of life.

The fact is that we are condemned to progress *ad infinitum*.

Not only are we just beginning, but we shall always be just beginning, as far as we can see ahead. On the horizon are further changes and adaptations; on the horizon is the hope that we will be wise enough to make the right choices, with the courage and vitality called for by the ceaseless pursuit of progress and the acceptance of every challenge on the way.

Chapter **4** **The Basic Minimums**

On this road where there can be no more stopping are a number of necessary tasks which must be attended to without delay. Neglecting them would endanger the impetus we have acquired, perhaps would slow it down irreparably.

And here we encounter a basic difficulty which has become more and more acute in reecnt years. It is created by the political regime under which we have lived for over a century.

We are a nation within a country where there are two nations. For all the things we mentioned earlier, using words like "individuality," "history," "society," and "people," are also the things one includes under the word "nation." It means nothing more than the collective will to live that belongs to any national entity likely to survive.

Two nations in a single country: this means, as well, that in fact there are *two majorities*, two "complete societies" quite distinct from each other trying to get along within a common framework. That this number puts us in a minority position makes no difference: just as a civilized society will never condemn a little man to feel inferior beside a bigger man, civilized relations among nations demand that they treat each other as equals in law and in fact.

Now we believe it to be evident that the hundred-year-old framework of Canada can hardly have any effect other than to create increasing difficulties between the two parties insofar as their mutual respect and understanding are concerned, as well as impeding the changes and progress so essential to both.

It is useless to go back over the balance sheet of the century just past, listing the advantages it undoubtedly has brought us and the obstacles and injustices it even more unquestionably has set in our way.

The important thing for today and for tomorrow is that both sides realize that this regime has had its day, and that it is a matter of urgency either to modify it profoundly or to build a new one.

As we are the ones who have put up with its main disadvantages, it is natural that we also should be in the greatest hurry to be rid of it; the more so because it is we who are menaced most dangerously by its current paralysis.

Primo Vivere

Almost all the essential tasks facing us risk being jeopardized, blocked, or quietly undone by the sclerosis of Canadian institutions and the open or camouflaged resistance of the men who manipulate them.

First, we must secure once and for all, in accordance with the complex and urgent necessities of our time, the safety of our collective "personality." This is the distinctive feature of the nation, of this majority that we constitute in Quebec—the only true fatherland left us by events, by our own possibilities, and by the incomprehension and frequent hostility of others.

The prerequisite to this is, among other things, the power for unfettered action (which does not exclude co-operation) in fields as varied as those of citizenship, immigration, and employment; the great instruments of "mass culture"—films, radio, and television; and the kind of international relations that alone permit a people to breathe the air of a changing and stimulating world, and to learn to see beyond itself. Such relations are especially imperative for a group whose cultural connections in the world are as evident and important as ours.

Our collective security requires also that we settle a host of questions made so thorny by the present regime that each is more impossible than the next. Let us only mention as examples the integrity of Quebec's territory, off-shore rights, the evident inacceptibility of an institution like the Supreme Court, and Quebec's need to be able to shape freely what we might term its internal constitution.

That collective personality which constitutes a nation also cannot tolerate that social security and welfare—which affect it daily in the most intimate ways—should be conceived and directed from outside. This relates to the oft-repeated demand for the repatriation of old-age pensions, family allowances, and, when it comes into being, medicare.

By the same token, and even more so, it relates to the most obvious needs of efficiency and administrative responsibility. In this whole vast area there are overlapping laws, regulations, and organizations whose main effect is to perpetuate confusion and, behind this screen, to paralyze change and progress.

The Madhouse

Mutatis mutandis, we find similar situations with equally disastrous results in a multitude of other areas: the administration of justice, jurisdiction in fields such as insurance, corporations, bankruptcies, financial institutions, and, in a general way, all economic activities which have become the most constant preoccupations of all men today and also the aspect of society in which modern states have seen their sphere of action grow most dramatically in the last couple of generations.

On this point, here is how the C.S.N., the F.T.Q., and the U.C.C.* describe the situation in their joint memorandum to the Quebec Legislature's Constitutional Committee:

The fact that certain economic tools belong to the federal government, while other powers whose exercise also influences economic life belong to the provinces, creates a difficult problem in the rational planning of economic activity in general. Thinking in terms of a more advanced socialization than that which we know today, this situation, along with opportunity given one government to thwart the actions of other, may lead to conflict, and is in any case of such a nature that it could, at these two levels of government, result in impotence in attacking the economic problems of the country with any kind of resolution or efficiency. Any duplication of institutions should be avoided, moreover, if it leads to a duplication of costs. This situation should demand our attention all the more urgently because of the fact that already (for example, in agriculture) laws and regulations at the two levels of government, and especially their application, because of their overlapping, their duplication, their superimposition of their lack of co-ordination, cause many grave difficulties and are often most prejudicial to the citizens involved, especially those of Quebec in view of our lagging behind in a number of areas.

Here again let us limit ourselves to citing the minimums established by the most complete studies of recent years. And so,

*C.S.N. is the *Confédération des Syndicats Nationaux* (Confederation of National Trade Unions) and F.T.Q. is the *Fédération des Travailleurs du Québec* (Quebec Labour Federation). These are the two largest central labour bodies in the province. The U.C.C. is the *Union Catholique des Cultivateurs,* a major farm organization sometimes known in English as the Catholic Farmers' Union or the Farmers' Catholic Union.

back to those three organizations and the way in which they define these minimums in the cautious conclusion of their memorandum:

The Quebec government should exercise its powers by giving direction to the economy, rationalizing its marginal industries, developing secondary industry, etc. The government of Quebec should promote an economic policy frankly favourable to its own population and more demanding vis-à-vis the capitalist interests, for it is not enough only to appear to govern in favour of the people in this sector. In particular, the Quebec government must obtain the greatest advantages and royalties it can possibly extract from the exploitation of natural resources, taking account of the reasonable limits of this kind of policy. Activity just as intense and equally devoted to the interests of the people must spread through all departments responsible for economic matters, notably agriculture, industry, and commerce, and so forth.

This outline, which is necessarily incomplete ("and so forth"), hints at a program immediately acceptable to everyone, but it poses at once the question of means.

A Strong State

How can it be carried out? Let us mention only what is clearly obvious. Order must be re-established in the chaos of a governmental structure created at a time when it was impossible to foresee the scientific and technical revolution in which we now are caught up, the endless changes it demands, the infinite variety of things produced, the concentration of enterprises, the crushing weight that the greatest of these impose on individual and collective life, the absolute necessity of having a state able to direct, co-ordinate, and above all humanize this infernal rhythm.

In this up-dating of political structures that are completely overtaxed by an economic role they cannot refuse to play, the action demanded of the Quebec government, to be specific, would require at the very least new jurisdictions over industrial and commercial corporations, fiduciary and savings institutions, and all the internal agencies of development and industrialization, as well as the power to exercise a reasonable control over the movement and investment of our own capital.

So as not to belabour the obvious, we shall mention only for the record the massive transfer of fiscal resources that would be needed for all the tasks this State of Quebec should undertake in our name—not counting the tasks it already has, tasks that daily grow more out of proportion to its inadequate means: *i.e.,* the insatiable needs of education, urban problems without number, and the meagreness or tragic non-existence of the tools of scientific and industrial research.

Very sketchily, this would seem to be the basic minimum of change that Quebec should force the present Canadian regime to accept in order to reach both the collective security and the opportunity for progress which its best minds consider indispensable.

We could certainly add to the list. But nothing could be struck from it easily.

For us, this is, in fact, a true minimum.*

Chapter **5** **The Blind Alley**

But we would be dreaming if we believed that for the rest of the country our minimum can be anything but a frightening maximum, completely unacceptable even in the form of bare modifications or, for that matter, under the guise of the constitutional reform with which certain people say they are willing to proceed with.

Not only the present attitude of the federal government, but also the painful efforts at understanding made by the opposition parties and reactions in the most influential circles in English Canada all give us reason to expect that our confrontation will grow more and more unpleasant.†

From a purely revisionist point of view, our demands would seem to surpass both the best intentions displayed by the "other majority" and the very capacity of the regime to make concessions without an explosion.

Cf. Appendix 1, "Some Varieties of Special Status."
†*Cf.* Appendix 2, "Neo-Centralization."

If we are talking only of revision, they will tell us, our demands would lead to excessive weakening of that centralized state which English Canada needs for its own security and progress as much as we need our own State of Quebec. And they would be right.

And further, they could ask us—with understandable insistence—what in the world our political representatives would be doing in Ottawa taking part in debates and administrative acts whose authority and effectiveness we intend so largely to eliminate within Quebec.

If Quebec were to begin negotiations to revise the present frame of reference, and persisted in this course, it would not be out of the woods in the next hundred years. But by that time it is most likely that there would be nothing left worth talking about of the nation that is now trying to build a homeland in Quebec.

During the long wait we would soon fall back on the old defensive struggle, the enfeebling skirmishes that make one forget where the real battle is, the half-victories that are celebrated between two defeats, the relapse in to divisive federal-provincial electoral folly, the sorry consolations of verbal nationalism and, above all, ABOVE ALL ELSE—this must be said, and repeated, and shouted if need be—above all the incredible "split-level" squandering of energy, which certainly is for us the most disastrous aspect of the present regime.

And as for this waste of energy, English Canada suffers from it, too. And there, too, the best minds have begun to realize this fact, let there be no doubt of that.

Two Paralyzed Majorities

For the present regime also prevents the English-speaking majority from simplifying, rationalizing, and centralizing as it would like to do certain institutions which it, too, realizes are obsolete. This is an ordeal which English Canada is finding more and more exhausting, and for which it blames to the exaggerated anxieties and the incorrigible intransigence of Quebec.

It is clear, we believe, that this frustration may easily become intolerable. And it is precisely among the most progressive and "nationalist" groups in English Canada, among those who are concerned about the economic, cultural, and political invasion from the United States, among those who are seeking the means to prevent the country from surrendering completely, that there is the greatest risk of a growing and explosive resentment toward Quebec for the reasons mentioned above.

And these are the very men among whom we should be able to find the best partners for our dialogue over the new order that must emerge.

We are seeking at last to carve out for ourselves a worthy and acceptable place in this Quebec which has never belonged to us as it should have. Facing us, however, a growing number of our fellow-citizens of the other majority are afraid of losing the homeland that Canada was for them in the good old days of the Empire, when they at least had the impression that they were helping to rule, and that it was all within the family. Today the centres of decision-making are shifting south of the border at a terrifying rate.

In this parallel search for two national securities, as long as the search is pursued within the present system or anything remotely resembling it, we can end up only with double paralysis. The two majorities, basically desiring the same thing—a chance to live their own lives, in their own way, according to their own needs and aspirations—will inevitably collide with one another repeatedly and with greater and greater force, causing hurts that finally would be irreparable.*

As long as we persist so desperately in maintaining—with spit and chewing gum or whatever—the ancient hobble of a federalism suited to the last century, the two nations will go on creating an ever-growing jungle of compromises while disagreeing more and more strongly on essentials.

This would mean a perpetual atmosphere of instability, of wrangling over everything and over nothing. It would mean the sterilization of two collective "personalities" which, having squandered the most precious part of their potential, would weaken each other so completely that they would have no other choice but to drown themselves in the ample bosom of "America."

---

*See in this connection the remarkable study by Jacques Parizeau, Appendix 3, "Quebec—Canada: A Blind Alley."

Chapter 6 The Way of The Future

We think it is possible for both parties to avoid this blind alley. We must have the calm courage to see that the problem can't be solved either by maintaining or somehow adapting the *status quo*. One is always somewhat scared at the thought of leaving a home in which one has lived for a long time. It becomes almost "consecrated," and all the more so in this case, because what we call "Confederation" is one of the last remnants of those age-old safeguards of which modern times have robbed us. It is therefore quite normal that some people cling to it with a kind of desperation that arises far more from fear than from reasoned attachment.

But there are moments—and this is one of them—when courage and calm daring become the only proper form of prudence that a people can exercise in a crucial period of its existence. If it fails at these times to accept the calculated risk of the great leap, it may miss its vocation forever, just as does a man who is afraid of life.

What should be conclude from a cool look at the crucial crossroads that we now have reached? Clearly that we must rid ourselves completely of a completely obsolete federal regime.

And begin anew.

Begin how?

The answer, it seems to us, is as clearly written as the question, in the two great trends of our age: that of the freedom of peoples, and that of the formation by common consent of economic and political groupings.

A Sovereign Quebec

For our own good, we must dare to seize for ourselves complete liberty in Quebec, the right to all the essential components of independence, *i.e.,* the complete mastery of every last area of basic collective decision-making.

This means that Quebec must become sovereign as soon as possible.

Thus we finally would have within our grasp the security of our collective "being" which is so vital to us, a security which otherwise must remain uncertain and incomplete.

Then it will be up to us, and us alone, to establish calmly, without recrimination or discrimination, the priority for which we are now struggling feverishly but blindly: that of our language and our culture.

Only then will we have the opportunity—and the obligation —to use our talents to the maximum in order to resolve without further excuses or evasions all the great problems that confront us, whether it be a negotiated protective system for our farmers, or decent treatment for our employees and workers in industry, or the form and evolution of the political structures we must create for ourselves.

In short, this is not for us simply the only solution to the present Canadian impasse; it also is the one and only common goal inspiring enough to bring us together with the kind of strength and unity we shall need to confront all possible futures —the supreme challenge of continuous progress within a society that has taken control of its own destiny.

As for the other Canadian majority, it will also find our solution to its advantage, for it will be set free at once from the constraints imposed on it by our presence; it will be at liberty in its own way to rebuild to its heart's desire the political institutions of English Canada and to prove to itself, whether or not it really wants to maintain and develop on this continent, an English-speaking society distinct from the United States.

– and a New Canadian Union

And if this is the case, there is no reason why we, as future neighbours, should not voluntarily remain associates and partners in a common enterprise; which would conform to the second great trend of our times: the new economic groups, customs unions, common markets, etc.

Here we are talking about something which already exists, for it is composed of the bonds, the complementary activities, the many forms of economic co-operation within which we have learned to live. Nothing says that we must throw these things away; on the contrary, there is every reason to maintain the framework. If we destroyed it, interdependent as we are, we would only be obliged sooner or later to build it up again, and then with doubtful success.

Now, it is precisely in the field of economics that we feel the pinch most painfully. In our outmoded constitutional texts and governmental structures, we flounder hopelessly over how to divided between our two states the powers, the agencies, and the means for action.

On this subject any expert with the slightest pretension to objectivity must certainly endorse the following statement by Otto Thur, Head of the Department of Economics at the University of Montreal (in a special edition of *Le Devoir,* June 30, 1967): "It is not the wording of a constitution that will solve problems [in the field of economics], but rather enlightened and consistent action, which brings about a progressive betterment of existing reality."

It seems to us, given a minimum of wisdom and, of course, self-interest—which should not be beyond the reach of our two majorities—that in the kind of association we are proposing we would have the greatest chance of pursuing jointly such a course of "enlightened and consistent action" worth more in economic affairs than all the pseudo-sacred documents with their ever-ambiguous inflexibility.

Such an association seems to us, in fact, made to measure for the purpose of allowing us, unfettered by obsolete constitutional forms, to pool our stakes with whatever permanent consultation and flexible adjustments would best serve our common economic interests: monetary union, common tariffs, postal union, administration of the national debt, co-ordination of policies, etc.

And nothing would prevent us from adding certain matters which under the present system have never had the advantage of frank discussion between equals: the question of minorities, for one; and also the questions of equal participation in a defence policy in proportion to our means, and a foreign policy that might, if conceived jointly, regain some of the dignity and dynamism that it has lost almost completely.*

*In this paragraph some people have felt obliged—and others have hastened—to find a far-too-strict limitation imposed on Quebec's sovereignty. This would indeed be true if we proposed really to include Defence and External Affairs in the areas of actual association. These two are among the most important means through which a people can express its personality. But such is not our proposal.

We are not sailing off into uncharted seas. Leaving out the gigantic model furnished by the evolution of the Common Market, we can take our inspiration from countries comparable in size to our own—Benelux or Scandinavia—among whom co-operation is highly advanced, and where it has promoted unprecedented progress in the member states without preventing any of them from continuing to live according to their own tradition and preferences.

Making History Instead of Submitting To It

To sum up, we propose a system that would allow our two majorities to extricate themselves from an archaic federal framework in which our two very distinct "personalities" paralyze each other by dint of pretending to have a third personality common to both.

This new relationship of two nations, one with its homeland in Quebec and another free to rearrange the rest of the country at will, would be freely associated in a new adaptation of the current "common-market" formula, making up an entity which could perhaps—and if so very precisely—be called a Canadian Union.

The future of a people is never born without effort. It requires that a rather large number of "midwives" knowingly make the grave decision to work at it. For apart from other blind forces, and apart from all the imponderables, we must believe that basically it is still men who make man's history.

What we are suggesting to those who want to listen is that we devote our efforts, together, to shape the history of Quebec in the only fitting direction; and we are certain that at the same time we shall also be helping the rest of the country to find better future of its own.

The highly conditional form in which it is couched, and the suggestion of preliminary studies, seem to us to indicate clearly enough that we were referring to the possibility of agreements which *might* be reached, agreements that would be strictly limited in nature (*e.g.*, joint general staffs? Certain common agencies abroad, such as commercial representatives?), which should not *a priori* be excluded in the free development of countries which are neighbours and partners. This is the sort of thing we had in mind below when we speak of these two distinct societies which "have a crying need now to give each other some breathing space, and to rediscover themselves, freely and without prejudice, creating little by little new points of contact as the need arises."

A Country that Is "Feasible"

We have nothing to fear but fear itself.
Franklin D. Roosevelt

The State gives form to everything
and becomes the keystone that
holds the national edifice together.
In this context, to be satisfied
with a piecemeal kind of power
is to be content with paralysis.
Editorial, Maintenant, *September 1967*

From Politics to Economics

What we must accomplish, then, is the full political liberty of Quebec, which we believe to be not only necessary but already inevitable.

And at the same time we must establish this liberty within the first and most obvious of our future and mutually dependent) relationships: the one we must create with the rest of Canada. The most concise and most exact formula to describe it is the one which came so naturally to the Member of the Quebec Legislative Assembly for Mercier, Robert Bourassa, in a speech on Associated Sovereign States to the Kiwanis Club of Montreal.

This association, essentially economic in nature, is no more than touched on in a few lines at the end of the "manifesto" you have just read.

How can we now spell it out as a valid hypothesis?

In the beginning, we must be content to establish a solid general outline for the required structure, without losing ourselves in the details of short-term or piecemeal economics, the factor always picked-on by the timid when they want to frighten themselves, and by "the others" when they want to frighten us.

Prepared with the help of some of Quebec's best minds in economic matters, the original version of our hypothesis was first reproduced in *Le Devoir*, and then distributed in modest mimeographed form, beginning October 1967.

Those who have read that original version will note that we have here made numerous minor changes and added several amplifications, some of these substantial ones. This was necessary, and we are sure such changes will continue to be increasingly necessary as we delve more deeply into this aspect of our new existence. As the work of the many able people our movement has attracted becomes more highly organized, such modifications are to be expected.

It will, however, be noted that we have made no fundamental changes.

This is simply because no one has yet found a weakness in the framework of our hypothesis. God knows it's been tried! And they're still trying. . . . But all these attacks, from the most sincere and honestly troubled to the most stupidly "terrorist" variety, have had the effect only of convincing us as the weeks go by of the overall worth of our proposals.

We are not in the position of refusing pretentiously to take into account any questions or objections, walling ourselves up within a new "possession of the truth." But it does seem clear to us that most of the arguments put forward to date by our opponents and by those who doubt in good faith are based mainly on an unavowed and perhaps even unconscious prejudice, which is one of our more insidious heritages from the past: the belief that we constitute a society and a people too incompetent and weak to accomplish what others do.

We are completely convinced of the contrary. We believe that for the first time Quebec is equipped with enough young and up-to-date leaders, aware of the historical—if fleeting—opportunity that is being offered us, to be able to meet successfully all the obstacles a people is certain to encounter on its way.

As for the "seasonal" objections, those short-term arguments (such as the learned calculations dealing with investments which might involve greater risks in October than in August . . . but less than in December!), they really deserve no more consideration than a shrug of the shoulders. Whether they are the product of ignorance or panic, or of a firm determination to frighten those "pea-soups," it is enough to note that they all bear on that very short term in which everyone is so vulnerable. Our hypothesis, on the contrary, is between short and long term, leaving time for awareness and preparation. It is based on the moment when a clear majority will have taken form to weigh and choose Quebec's new direction, with a government at its head that will represent its will and implement its decision as perfectly as possible.

You Can't Have One Without the Other

All this merely underlines the urgency of dealing quickly and effectively with the economic aspect of any major political project.

In all friendship, some have reproached us for dragging down, so to speak, the sacred subject of Quebec's liberty to a base level of material preoccupation. . . .

But is it not at this level that we spend most of life, without thinking much about it during ordinary times but with sudden and annoying anxiety when any disturbance occurs in this area?

Those who insist on keeping their heads in the clouds on this point will be the first to stumble.

Moreover, as Claude Ryan wrote in *Le Devoir* of June 30, 1967, "Economic policy is, in our times, the very essence of governmental action at every level." *To speak to the citizen of today about important political transformations, without taking into account the* homo economicus *that he incorporates, would be as factitious as undertaking a trip to the moon without checking the fuel in the rocket!*

If we study the laws, regulations, decisions, or judgements which are the manifestations of the exercise of power, without understanding the economic problems that have to be faced by authorities who are more or less aware and more or less capable, we certainly can come up with a list of texts and precedents, but we shall know nothing about contemporary society.

The world today is such that it is not possible to study economic problems without analyzing the organization of the state; nor is it possible to appreciate the structure and operation of the latter without becoming involved in the problem of economics.

Bernard Chenot, *Economic Organization of the State*

Chapter **1** The Association

> *There must be an English-Canadian nation (not just
> a collection of English-speaking provinces) in partner-
> ship with the French-Canadian nation. . . . It is time
> that we realized the demands of French Canada,
> recognizing them as normal human demands, and
> making the same claims ourselves.*
>
> *Gad Horowitz, McGill University*

> *There certainly exists a tendency which impels peoples
> to form ever-larger economic groups. But one sees in
> the world no equivalent tendency toward more ex-
> tended political units.*
>
> *John Kenneth Galbraith, Weekend, 1967*

I THE GAMBLE

The take-off is a gamble.

In any important enterprise that a people decides to undertake, there is of necessity an element of calculated risk.

Ours seems to us quite reasonable. We firmly believe that
the association of equals we propose soon will be acceptable to
the rest of the country.

It will be not only acceptable, but even desirable, because of
the alternative prospect of a special status that would be grabbed
by Quebec, bit by bit, until the federal state became a kind of
constitutional freak in perpetual danger of disintegration.

In short, this other gamble—for it also is a gamble, this
cacophony of "special *status quo*" suggestions—seems to us to
present a picture of distracted leaders hiding behind promises of
verbal accomplishments, which grow noisier as they grow more
incoherent. It is a bet placed on intellectual mediocrity and fear
of change, clinging to that established order under which evolution is placing a time-bomb.

The risk in this other gamble is that, with our eyes closed,
we may come to lose forever the fresh impetus of a people that
has been fooled too often; we risk ruining what may be its
supreme chance to live at last in the secure pursuit of a future
that is not only acceptable but exhilarating.

We, on the other hand, are proposing the gamble that *should* be made and stayed with and won, with our eyes open: open to the evolution of reality, open to the fundamental interests of Quebec, to the many solutions that the world today can suggest to us, and open, of course, to the behaviour and reactions of English Canada.

*"Over my dead body"**

From English Canada we have so far heard only objections— and they have been very quick and very loud.

Nothing could be more natural. Faced with any clear design for change (which upsets so many things, even if at heart one knows it is inevitable), one's first reaction is invariably negative. The first thing one says is "Never!"

The most categorical English-speaking "Never!" (and one of the most violently instinctive) came *post-haste* in September 1967 from Eric Kierans.

He began, unfortunately, by falsifying the meaning of our alternative. He did this quite knowingly, describing it repeatedly and unqualifiedly as "separatist," that word of disintegration which is used in English only through clenched teeth, a sign that discussion is useless.

This mood of morbid exultation is a preparation for the plunge into catastrophe. Our proposition having been misrepresented in this way, it can be denounced loudly as utterly unacceptable. It becomes, tragically and instantly, the end of Canada as an entity. The rest of the country, Kierans said, rather than accept this, would turn its back upon us forever and commit *hara-kiri*, slashing itself to pieces, to fall bit by bit into the old north-south axis and American annexation. Which would, he added, allow it to get rid of the twenty per cent or so "premium" we have paid in cost of living for the last century just to keep the country separate.

This was the sledge hammer answer, the blow you get in early in the hope of knocking out your adversary in the first round.†

But he was a little premature, we feel, in nominating himself

---

*In English in the original.

†After Kierans' outburts, the rest of the first round was marked mostly by a remarkable "operation" against Quebec, of which you will find a short analysis in Appendix 7, "Operation Panic."

as the spokesman for an English Canada that might in two or three years' time be able to see a progressive rallying of Quebec opinion, the formation of a majority able to combine an unshakeable firmness with a polite insistence on speaking calmly, an insistence on bringing this crisis to a final solution which would provide relief to both sides as well as the certainty that the future was, after all, possible.

Because, for one thing, this "premium," the price we all have paid to maintain a country distinct from the United States, was not paid because Quebec has pretty blue eyes.

But When You Think It Over . . .

It was above all the society of English Canada, and especially Ontario (the results are there to prove it), that wanted a Canada and built its whole economy around this very "premium." The latter, in fact, is quite simply the result of the Canadian-American border: here flourish the finance and industry in which our share is so small. The great American interests were forced, in order to occupy the market, to extend their activities here and there north of the border, but again mainly in southern Ontario.

The disappearance of this border would mean, likely sooner than later, the fall of Ontario to the stature of a second-class state, and a stagnation in the rest of English Canada comparable to that of the American South.

Because of its present course and its privileged situation along the Great Lakes, close to the vibrant Midwest, Ontario would probably end up by fitting without too much trouble into the American industrial machine. In the same way, unless we refuse to allow it, Montreal and the St. Lawrence Valley down to Quebec will become the natural extension of the gigantic megalopolis extending from Chicago east along both sides of the Seaway.

But what about New Brunswick? And Prince Edward Island? And Manitoba? And even Alberta, whose unexpected good fortune rests on the position carefully accorded it by the federal government because of its oil production?

Far from the more dynamic centres of the continental economy, these provinces would have nothing to look forward to but a long stagnation, like so many northern Alabamas.

And whatever else happened, a whole circle of prominent business leaders, who are very big fish in the tiny Canadian pond, in the event of annexation would have to undergo the traumatic experience of becoming small fry in the ocean.

To this would be added the dubious delights of the military draft, participation in present and future Vietnams, and all the racial and other strife that American society has brought upon itself.

And even before English Canada's disappearance into the Great Whole, it would, by refusing an understanding with Quebec, be obliged to put the axe to a national entity cherished by many English-Canadians as much as we cherish our own. This is certainly true for innumerable people in Ontario and for many Maritimers and even, behind W. A. C. Bennett's secessionism—a pose as amusing as it is profitable—for more British Columbians than one might think. . . .

Returning to the economic side of things, let us add that such a break-up would coincide with loss of the Quebec market, which is rather important to the rest of the country. It is true that we export to other parts of Canada thirty-one per cent of our manufactured goods (our revenue from raw materials obviously remaining relatively safe under any equitable regime) but is equally true to say, as Robert Bourassa said in other days: "We import *so much* from the other Canadian provinces, and especially Ontario!" (The expression "so much" is a discreet way of saying that, with a ratio of two dollars in purchases for every dollar in sales, Quebec is, from this point of view, an extremely profitable market for the rest of Canada.)* In other words, the balance of trade is very profitable to the latter. This is not the kind of *business*† that practical minds would accept losing or jeopardizing, unless an *entente* with Quebec were really unthinkable.

This is why we think we should win our gamble, if it were backed by the vigour of a friendly Quebec whose nerves at last had grown steady.

For we must not forget that while our Quebec majority was

---

*These figures are necessarily approximate, as there are still no complete and reliable statistics on the internal flow of trade. We had at first—with the support of certain experts—set the disproportion at three dollars, to one dollar. It was suggested however, that we reduce this to a minimum of two to one, until we are able to define the exact dimensions of an imbalance whose existence and size are clearly obvious.

†In English in the original.

acquiring a clearer picture of itself, a parallel process of psychological development, painful but inevitable, would necessarily be taking place in the other majority. At its completion that process should allow us to sit at the same table without too great a gap between us.

II THE PROJECT

On that table, we propose that Quebec should lay a project for association which would include: a monetary union and a "common market," along with their logical complement, the coordination of fiscal policies.

Some, at one extreme, will tend to see in this association very serious inmpediments to that independence of which they have dreamed so intensely, that it is, understandably, hard for them to view it as being anything but absolute and complete. The slightest amputation seems to them to make it a thing unbearably flawed and suddenly much less worthy of their enthusiasm. The point is this: we as a people have all the means we need, but not enough that we can afford to be carried away by mirages or by conditions that are no longer applicable.

The limitations we have mentioned are very real and no less substantial. If they were not, there would be no need to talk about "association."

And yet they are very much the kind of constraint that a number of countries have had to impose on themselves, countries which were close geographic neighbours but had to "come a long way" in order to find each other. Especially in old Europe, covered with stitched-up wounds, still filled with bloody memories, they are reaching laboriously (and still without having seriously touched on monetary matters) the kind of results which for us could be from the beginning our contract of association.

The fact is, they have had to come to terms with an evident truth of our times, as we will have to do: from the viewpoint of trade among nations, and the relative stability they must have in relation to each other, some ancient elements of sovereignty are more of a hinderance than an advantage. They are less and less useful in defending economic positions of any importance, tending rather to complicate, riddle with pitfalls, and undermine the co-operation and interrelation that increasingly have become the prerequisites for continued growth.

(It is of course extremely important to keep in your hands all controls and to create or recover all the essential powers that affect internal development and allow a national society to ensure that it is being *served* by the economy which must maintain it and in large measure, shape its life.)

At the other extreme are those who will insist on seeing in this project of association a confirmation of their own inferiority complexes. They will find in it only an admission of all the weaknesses and inadequacies of which they never tire of reminding us, thus supporting and propagating an incurable defeatism.

They will say: "You see? It's no use pretending to be what we're not. Isn't it a proof that we aren't up to any great decision if we have to have a common currency and common tariffs?"

Well, let us just point out that we should not be so morbid as to list nothing but our failings, unless we feel that we haven't the courage for a real confrontation. We also must assess coldly our own strong points, especially those which correspond to the other side's weaknesses.

We have already noted the more than substantial advantages that the Quebec market brings the rest of the country. A customs union, therefore, should be quite attractive to it!

As for currency, the proposal to maintain monetary unity is for some critics no more than a chance to expound upon the inevitable difficulties that creation of a Quebec currency would bring: highly probable instability in the early stages, the flight of capital, an end to free exchange, devaluation. As far as I know, no one, on the other hand, has gone so far as to say it would be impossible, for such a statement would be ludicrously false.

But it would be equally ludicrous to forget that, if there were two currencies and if ours should run inevitably into early difficulties, the other would also be quickly hit by the backlash and undermined in its turn; and as it waited for the final break-up, a separated English Canada itself would have a sorry-looking dollar. . . .*

*Early in October 1967, D. H. Fullerton, a prominent financial expert who has acted on many occasions as adviser to the Quebec government and Hydro-Quebec, wrote me an open letter: "If there were no monetary union, the Quebec dollar would depreciate more than the [new] Canadian dollar. If I were asked to estimate these

Finally, there are still others who, not content with only imagining the ideal world as they conceive it, insist on shoving us into it first, whether we like it or not.

Their splendid whimsy holds that political federalism is necessarily a superior form of civilization and consequently is endowed with irresistible attractions.

"Since we're talking about association," they say, "we are really taking a path that leads inevitably to new federalism. So why leave the existing structure if we're only going to go back to it later on?"

This notion of a fated return to the old system (which, at best, is simply the safe rationalization of the horse terrified at the prospect of leaving a familiar stable) is somehow depicted as announcing a new age. In terms as noble as they are unrealistic, this group tries to hasten a development which they would like to think is unavoidable in the various European associations. They even attribute to man a certain sublime will to excel himself—without, unfortunately, consulting man!

They seek in the individual a creature ready to plunge into the homogenization of peoples, a creature who is de-nationalized, almost disembodied, who gives thought only to his noble, generic title of "man," and, with exemplary wisdom, worries only about socio-economic progress (the "real problem," as they like to say, making faces at all the others).

We, too, in a way; but we don't expect to live until the twenty-second century. And this nationalism that they would like to root out by underlining only its excesses can also (a fact they forget) be called *patriotism*. Under this beautiful name it still is, and will long remain, the mainspring of cultural vitality and of any significant progress made by the families of man.

Whatever was thought or hoped for at the outset of the European unions, this is the most obvious conclusion we can

results, I would see the Quebec dollar going down to $0.70, and the Canadian dollar to $0.80, expressed in American dollars. A new monetary equilibrium would finally be established at these lower rates, but the transitional period would be full of serious difficulties." So far as I know, no other expert has publicly risked an estimate of the probabilities in this field. Fullerton's illustrates simultaneously the mutual gain *for the two countries* of the formula we propose, and the fact that by holding out despite our disadvantage for the first few years, an independent Quebec could if necessary live without our formula.

draw from them today. It becomes more and more clear, in fact, that it is the *Europe des patries*, the "Europe of the fatherlands," as de Gaulle baptized it, which will survive infinitely after all the "paper United States" the federalists were forming feverishly, while berating the General.*

Now let us now have a look at the essential framework–without, as we said before, going into all the details–of the association we propose between a Sovereign Quebec and the rest of Canada.

a / Monetary Union

What is required in this case is a transitional agreement.

During the first years of separation, our two states will have a great number of extensive and delicate adjustments to make.

There is no definite denial of a provision in these, if it should be necessary, of the dissolution of the present monetary structure and the creation of a Quebec currency, along with the establishment of the agencies and the complex policies that would go with it.

But, in our opinion, nothing says that this must happen. It seems, in fact, highly advisable, at least temporarily and in the evident interest of both parties, to spare ourselves this heavy additional burden, along with the passing but painful and unsettling effects it would cause to all concerned.

For example, there is no good reason for precipitately severing the extremely intimate relationship between the two great financial markets of Montreal and Toronto. However dubious their method of operation may be in many respects, their complementary magnetic effects always have been the channel for most of the country's resources and jointly have ensured their distribution. Again, unless we should be forced to do so, why destroy this financial mechanism by a monetary break-away, when the normal evolution of a common market inevitably would lead us toward setting it up again sooner or later?

The objective, of course, can be made that this would serve only to maintain the domination now exercised by Toronto over its Montreal "satellite." At first this would be true. And it is no less true that, except in the excesses of public eloquence, it is impossible overnight to replace all our old shortcomings by new and miraculous achievements.

*See Appendix 5, "Association of Sovereign States," Principles.

The important thing is to know whether we thus are condemning ourselves to perpetuating the excessive burden of our dependence on the Toronto financial world. In fact, we are doing nothing of the kind. Quebec and its Montreal market will become "masters in their own house" on condition that our state has the will power to work out an efficient policy and creates the means for doing so. It suffices in this connection to mention the enormous influence that our *Caisse de Dépôts* already has acquired over a market in which it appeared only two years ago, and to add the results that would quickly follow on an adequate co-ordination and an intelligent use of our main financial institutions—especially those in the co-operative sector—within the framework of modern legislation and the powers that political sovereignty would have returned completely to our hands.

(To give an idea of the present size of our public "agencies" and co-ops in this area and, even more important, of their phenomenal rate of growth, here is a rough survey done late in 1967.)

	TOTAL ASSETS	YEARLY GROWTH
PUBLIC		
Caisse de Dépôts	$1,000,000,000 ± (in two years from now)	$250,000,000
Caisses Populaires (and other groups: *Caisses d'épargne,* Credit Union League, etc.)	$1,750,000,000 ±	$200,000,000

With an annual growth rate of about $250 million, the co-operative sector alone handles almost a third of the personal savings of Quebec, valued at the moment at $800 to $850 million.

Finally, let us again recall—and it is not wrong to insist, given the strength of the illusions held by some on this subject—what a narrow margin for manoeuvre is retained in monetary matters by nations subject to the interdependence that is the rule in advanced economic systems.

It becomes more and more obvious that they must give up the old "absolutist" concept of independence. This is true for

all countries, whatever they are or have been. The successive
discomfitures of the Pound Sterling are those of a Great Britain
unable to "re-cycle" itself successfully in its new role as an
ex-great power; while the increasing nervousness of the U.S.A.
over the dollar is that of the new super-power in a world where
the unquestioned hegemonies of yesterday are no longer think-
able.

This applies even more to countries which enter into economic association with each other. As a façade, each of them
presently keeps its own currency, its central bank, and all the
apparatus of monetary self-determination. It would have been
miraculous if the franc, the mark, the lire, etc. (with which are
involved in each country so many agencies, the careers of emi-
nent specialist careers, and even, undeniably, a whole slice of
national culture), were to come to any easy acceptance of a
monetary esperanto!

But behind the façade, the realities of economic association
interlace and link together to currencies and central banks as
inextricably as is the case with production and marketing. If the
mark catches a cold, the franc also starts coughing and the lire
begins at once to feel a little ill. . . .

We, who at the moment have neither agencies nor special-
ists nor any cultural patrimony depending on an indigenous
"piastre," have nothing to gain by insisting on an attribute of
independance which evolution is in the process of turning into
a liability.

This is why we believe that Quebec should propose to the
rest of Canada a treaty for monetary union with a duration of
five years—at the same time a trial period and a transitional
period.

If at the end of this initial period, the agreement were found
to be sufficiently valid to warrant renewal, we would have
created for once an original model which would be sure to in-
spire imitation by any number of countries.

It is quite obvious, and this calls for more common sense
than imagination, that the existing monetary organization would
lend itself admirably to this kind of agreement.

The Bank of Canada is a public corporation whose capital
($5 million) is under the jurisdiction of the federal Minister of
Finance.

Two associated states can decide to make a joint venture of
it in the following eminently practical way:

—The Board of Directors (twelve members) becomes a joint one including both co-shareholding states;

—To the federal Deputy-Minister of Finance, who already sits in the Council without having a vote, is added his opposite number from Quebec;

—It becomes statutory that the positions of Governor—President and Deputy Governor—Vice President should alternate between officials from the two states;

—A proportional distribution of top positions is worked out over a reasonable period of adaptation.

And this Bank issues and supervises a common currency, jointly administers reserves and national debts and protects the stability of the two states.

b / Common Market

Here we need no long explanations.

We must profit by one of the main, driving concepts sweeping the world today.

In the West we can already find three applications of it: the common market of Central America (Salvador, Guatemala, Honduras, and Nicaragua); Benelux (The Netherlands, Belgium, and Luxemburg), which pioneered the formula; and by far the best known, the great common market of the Six in Europe (France, West Germany, Italy, and Benelux) created in 1957 by the Treaty of Rome. (There is also the integration which the countries of the Scandinavian Union have carried out progressively and unobtrusively, with remarkable success.)

This is the means by which all these neighbours, formerly highly suspicious of each other and in some cases deeply hostile, have succeeded, to their great advantage, in setting up common economic structures.

Now, the same process that has brought them closer to each other can prevent us—and, most especially, the rest of the country—from drifting apart in an irreparable division.

The heart of a common market is the customs union, which forbids member states to levy tariffs on goods exchanged between them, and requires the maintenance of a common tariff barrier against non-members (See Appendix 5, "Association of Sovereign States.")

In this context our two states would simply continue the present absence of frontiers for purposes of reciprocal import-export exchanges.

It should be noted carefully that this in no way implies a pure and simple continuation of the *status quo*. It involves the conclusion of another agreement—in this case for a long, initial period of at least twenty years. This calls for prior negotiation, during which it would be possible to rectify certain anomalies. For example, why could we not correct the total lack of protection in the metropolitan market of Montreal, which is our main outlet for farm produce, as part of a comprehensive "rehabilitation" of our agriculture?

New or amended tariffs on goods from outside would, of course, be set through regular consultation between the two ministers concerned, who could come to agreement on the advantages and disadvantages of any changes.*

In this matter, as in the fiscal co-ordination which is its corollary (and which could well replace the "fiscal jungle" dictated to us in the autumn of 1966 from Ottawa), it would be necessary to set up mixed permanent committees of officials appointed by both states. Also obviously needed would be a well-integrated group under a secretary-general, forming the highest administrative authority of the association, as well as a court of arbitration.

To this structure would be added, following complementary agreements, other agencies of a similar nature to deal with questions needing co-ordination or joint or parallel planning, *e.g.,* the Seaway, minorities, radio-television exchanges, citizenship, and mobility of labour. . . .

This would not exclude, of course, regular meetings of joint Councils of Ministers, and more or less frequent sessions delegations from the two parliaments.

And that's all.

And it's enough.

And it would be infinitely more healthy for the two parties concerned than a patched-up or so-called "renewed" federalism in which the shifting realities of two distinct societies (and most

---

*This resembles, but within the healthy equality of a partnership, one of the main demands of all those who seriously support a "special status," more or less patched together though it might be.

We must admit that in our present situation Quebec sometimes suffers from a tariff policy elaborated without consultation and for the benefit of other provinces. The least that Quebec can demand is to take part in the making of tariff policy so as to safeguard its own interests. Robert Bourassa, September 27, 1967.

of these realities are still undefined at this very moment!) would again be crammed into prefabricated judicial structures instead of being first examined and lived with.

For these two societies have a crying need now to give each other some breathing space, and to rediscover themselves, freely and without prejudice, creating little by little new points of contact as the need arises.

Chapter **2** **The Transition Period**

In the long term we are all dead. (J. M. Keynes)

How will the sovereign State of Quebec manage to move successfully through the inevitable period of transition that will follow its appearance?

We have already said, and it is quite obvious, that this stage is situated in the "middle term," that is, in the only perspective in which we can seriously evaluate the overall chances of any society.

Let us say that in roughly three years our chances will be those of a people that has calmly chosen the direction of its future and given itself leaders capable of making the first steps as judiciously as possible.

At this moment in the future, then, we have already come through our early confusion and short-term panic; we are well past the days when every "well-informed" appeal automatically triggered a series of cautionary pontifical sermons addressed by certain editors to their too-restive flocks . . . the days when Eric Kierans could launch his incredible flailing attacks on the "uninstructed."*

After a few short years, with the democratic participation of a majority of citizens who will have made their decision

---

*In the fall of 1967, first version of what constitutes the second part of this book was sometimes called a "reply to Mr. Kierans." That resulted from the fact that we were then in the heat of his brief "terrorist" compaign. But the element of "reply" was really only very incidental in texts that had been put together before all the fuss began. The few traces remaining in this chapter may have a documentary interest.

calmly, we must, then, foresee a transitional period which should last two or three more years.

In order to be ready for this period it would seem that there are only three conditions that must be fulfilled without fail. None of them appears excessively difficult.

I FINANCING THE STATE

In achieving its political liberty, Quebec naturally will take back complete control of its fiscal resources.

The portion of these now going to Ottawa (twenty-five per cent of regular federal revenue) is calculated currently at over $2 billion plus our annual contribution of about $350 million to the old age pension fund (1967-8).

If we add these to the revenues now collected within the State of Quebec, does our fiscal repatriation allow us to satisfy our major collective needs?

If we can count on a basic minimum of maturity and competence in the required places, the reply is undoubtedly yes.

As a simple clue to the substantial economies which certainly can be made under a host of headings, and which could be transferred to new uses in Quebec, here is a quick survey of "senior" federal departments and agencies which are either totally or largely redundant, Quebec having had to set up parallel equipment or wait until everyone else was served: Agriculture, Fisheries, Energy, Mines and Resources, Indian Affairs and Northern Development, National Parks (there are none in Quebec), Forests, Revenue, Justice, Manpower, Labour, Health and Welfare, Industry; the Atlantic Development Board, the Board of Grain Commissioners, the Farm Credit Corporation, the Insurance Department, the Bureau of Statistics, and the Royal Canadian Mounted Police who are the provincial police in eight provinces). . . .

And finally—and this should be emphasized most strongly—the trio formed by the National Research Council, Canadian Patents and Development (its economically strategic subsidiary), and Atomic Energy of Canada. These constitute a vital circuit of research agencies built outside our borders and totally non-existent in Quebec. Our participation in them (except for a trickle of subsidies to universities) has a maximum value of just about zero.

In addition to all these "national" agencies, for which we

would no longer have to pour money down the drain (as is largely the case at present), let us not forget that we also would see an end to the infernal squandering of money that has gone on shamelessly in Ottawa for years and years, at the expense of Quebec taxpayers as well as taxpayers everywhere.

This happy tradition of muddle-and-waste, which has become accentuated with the increasing need to justify the excess of "fiscal fat" inherited from the Second World War, unfortunately is far from being common knowledge. Ottawa is so far away that its stupidities escape us or leave us almost as indifferent as those of a foreign capital. . . .

But in early December of 1967, the Minister of Revenue, in announcing "austerity" measures, happened suddenly to lift a few corners of the veil. Consider what this meant!

Edgar Benson succeeded at one stroke in cutting in half the increases *normally* anticipated in civil-service personnel. It seems there were outraged cries in all departments, but never fear! Things are still quite comfortable. This was a reduction to five thousand new employees from an annual rate of increase that for years had been established at ten to fifteen thousand! And this is an administration where we know very well that our share of the better jobs still is consistently below fifteen per cent.

At the same time they again reduced from 107,000 to the nice round figure of 100,000 the oddly elastic strength of our pseudo-defence forces. This gave everyone the opportunity to remember that from a military point of view the Canadian mini-power now has been straining for a whole generation to be something it is not, at an average cost of $2 billion a year.

In the host of pluses and minuses that would have to be dealt with in our new division of tasks and resources, there is one great gap which shows up at once. It is that of the equalization payments which a sovereign Quebec obviously no longer would receive, and which must therefore be compensated for in some other way.

These sums (equalization payments classed as "general" or "special") which Quebec receives as compensation for tax revenues which are lower than in richer parts of the country, amount at present to a maximum of some $340 million a year.

With most indecent haste, and with as much malicious enjoyment as lack of deliberation, a variety of defenders of the present obsolete system pounced on this fact.

They forgot the rule of commonsense under which, if such a gap appears in a total fiscal picture, one must look around to see if it cannot reasonably be filled by taking what is needed from somewhere else.

(This was, alas, the case with Kierans, who hastened to treat this minus as an absolute, spreading it over five years to obtain an even more terrifying row of zeros!)

We shall see that it is not at all difficult, without even touching on those priority projects which must at all cost be maintained, to fill the gap completely.

Here are three areas where savings can be made for this purpose (and there are certainly others):

a / Defence: $500 million (twenty-five per cent of federal spending).

b / Foreign aid: $75 million (again twenty-five per cent).

c / Excess collected on old-age security: $40 million (this is the only important fiscal area where Quebec clearly pays more than it receives).

In all, this totals $615 million which can be re-employed as follows:

a / Loss of equalization payments to be made good: $350 million.

b / Defence: $150 million (to maintain and re-group our very modest forces and to "repatriate" and properly maintain the Quebec Citadelle and the Valcartier complex as well as St. Hubert, Bagotville, and the College Militaire Royal at St-Jean!).

c / Foreign aid: $40 million for the underdeveloped French-speaking areas of the world. There, too, people are starving.

d / Investments: $75 million (which will be mentioned again in the second part of this chapter).

To finance itself the state and its agencies (mainly Hydro-Quebec) also must be able to borrow.

Their needs, in the foreseeable future, will not, it is thought, have to exceed $450 million a year.

The *Caisse de Dépôts,* whose incredible growth-rate we mentioned in the previous chapter, has become in less than two years the main purchaser of government securities. It has reached a level in this field of $130 million a year, which by no means exhausts its resources.* If we add the various amortization funds and those of the *Commission des Accidents du Travail* (Workmen's Compensation) the public finance sector quite easily should be able to absorb some $225 million three years from now.

Even if we assume that the Toronto market will follow a *wait-and-see*† policy, it is hard to see how our Quebec institutions, with powerful impetus in an atmosphere of starting afresh, could not succeed in taking up $125 million a year. Again in the previous chapter, we pointed out the fact that the co-operative sector is growing as quickly as the public one.

And in recent times, thanks to loans better adapted to their means, the co-operative institutions have been growing into important bulwarks of the state.

Finally, with American investments secure, and the Seaway as well, the New York market would have no reason to behave abnormally, and the remainder could be taken up there with no more effort than at present; without any more effort, in any event, than that required of any borrower of good reputation, in the ever-changing climate of the *money-market*.†

II MAINTENANCE OF INVESTMENTS

Here, we believe, we must talk primarily about investment in industrial growth, the kind that most firmly promotes general economic progress in a society.

We might point out that this is the area where the "experts" are at their most numerous on every public platform.

This is doubtless because this is also the area in which the available figures are the most fluid and ambiguous, admirably adaptable to every mood, and especially to the darker and more menacing ones of paternalism.

A simple fact: we actually do not know, from year to year, the exact *net* total of these precious private investments for which we go begging with all the more frenzy because we are unable to channel in our own direction a respectable amount of our own capital.‡

*Since its annual growth-rate is $200 million, it is thus easily able to retain the means of maintaining other necessary purchases of a high priority: municipal and school debentures, industrial securities, etc.
†In English in the original.
‡Thus, some have pointed out sagely that between 1959 and 1967

A slightly less simple fact: the gap that we periodically notice widening between Quebec and Ontario, a source of pathological anguish, basically has nothing to do with our more-or-less total docility. It is merely a constant in our present situation. Fluctuations are mainly cyclical: Ontario, possessing the durable-goods industries, increases its lead in boom periods of large capital investment—and sees it narrow in slack periods, because primary and consumer-goods industries like those of Quebec are stronger at such times.

The constant factor is that Ontario still is moving faster and more strongly than Quebec in the main areas, and this really will not change until after a change in our respective situations in other areas, and then only after patient efforts. Until then, as long as Baptiste stays quiet, mum's the word: no federal cabinet minister is going to raise a finger! But let Baptiste begin to rumble and what was normal at once becomes *abnormal,* and the appeals to sweet reason and the cries of doom will begin to purr and terrorize respectively, each trying to outdo the other.

One final fact, and the most important one: the present drop in investment in Quebec, which is quite real, has nothing to do (and no one has yet brought forward the slightest proof to the contrary)* with political developments, but proceeds rather from factors such as the end of Expo, the slowing down of capital expenditures by the state, and following the Canadian-American agreement on automobiles which was superbly arranged

the gap is supposed to have widened in favour of Ontario. These years, however, were the most active (and even at that they were not *so* exceptional) that Quebec had known for a long time. And if we were to go back eight years before 1959, years which marked the apogee of a regime of "great stability" and of wide benevolence toward all foreign investors, the comparison between these two periods would certainly prove nothing whatsoever about the state of our collective situations.

*This reminds us of the already distant days when Kierans had all the head offices (CPR, CNR, Sun Life, etc.) moving higgledy-piggledy out of a sovereign Quebec, in his extreme haste forgetting just two little things: first, that unless new offices were opened at once for the new Quebec branches which would be needed, these enterprises would have trouble holding on to their operations and their clientele; and, second, that any company now opening in Quebec on a federal basis would have to do the same. For those who are bewitched by head-offices, this leaves a choice between size and quantity!

over the "hot line" between Toronto and Ottawa, the massive parachuting of some $300 to $400 million from the United States into Ontario.

And then, above all, there is the universal scarcity of capital, an undeniable condition that is growing more serious everywhere.

The United States is the best in point. All Canada – not only Quebec – is accustomed to beg its development from the United States, and then reproaching them for stifling our precious "initiative"! Well, we shall not be getting as much out of them from now on – unlike the good old days of investment by continuous transfusion. A host of problems as pressing as they are complex compels the American to watch the exit of capital from their country as never before; moreover, they now are more interested in a Europe in full resurgence than in their hat-in-hand neighbours.

This is why the $75 million in available fiscal assets, which we held in reserve in the first part of this chapter, likely will be called upon for our suggested purpose over a period extending well beyond the merely transitional stage.

That $75 million, then, would be adequate to assure much of the industrial growth that Quebec needs. Much more ample than what we have available at the moment, let it be said in passing. . . .

If the state uses this sum for five years or more to stimulate the rate of development, we will have by the same token a public sector that is at last strong and dynamic enough to form the backbone of this whole area of related activities, which we must make our own and retain within our national economic control.

It would be a valid hypothesis – workable in detail only after careful planning – to use this collective capital in the following ways:

1 / Forests

To bring about as soon as possible the necessary transformation of the old system of "concessions," a source of constant waste, involving exorbitant transport rates that make our costs prohibitive. It is only by lowering these costs that we can give a healthy incentive to capital to establish itself on a solid basis in this richest of our primary sectors. It also is only by putting an end to "concession" that our public forests really can become our own again.

Public investment then could be put to work in a rational way to create, whether alone or with the help of others, new uses for wood heretofore neglected in Quebec. We must remember that such flourishing industries, such as the manufacture of composite board from waste products, are non-existent or in the embryo stage in Quebec; and we should be the "kings of the forest"!

2 / Steel

This industry must be established, whatever steps we have to take, to get it under way. If only this can be started, and brought to completion!

3 / The Société Général de Financement

It must be given the stature and possibilities for which it was created.

It is still ridiculously far from having the authorized capital of $150 million which it was promised at the outset.* With its ten thousand employees it nonetheless has become in a very short space of time one of the greatest and most dynamic holding companies in Quebec. It controls the former Canadian Arsenals in Valcartier (which is making money, alas, like so many others, out of Vietnam!). It has set up, with European interests, the only recent industrial project designed for one of our less-favoured regions—a new paper mill in Charlevoix.

A sovereign Quebec must give it the means:

a / To accelerate the concentration and stimulate the specialization that are absolutely necessary in those older parts of our industry that date from the industrial revolution—textiles, clothing, furniture, and shoes. All these are dangerously vulnerable, although some thirty-five per cent *of our industrial employees* are in this area: people who would like very much to go on earning a living, and even a better living.

b / To move forward without delay to certain activities of the year 2000 which already are those of today; electronics

---

*In 1967, the Quebec State was able to provide it with no more than the relatively microscopic pittance of $5 million for two years.

among others, that limitless universe which has been but barely touched. Here a well-endowed *Société Générale de Financement* would need only to join forces with the Hydro research complex, and there would be no danger of us becoming mere "hewers of wood and drawers of water" in the world of the future, the world of satellites, for example, of which we hear so much, and which now are forming new constellations in our skies.

All these accomplishments would also allow us to clarify for some time to come the respective roles of the public, mixed, and private sectors, ridding the latter in its own part of the economy of certain obsolete administrative or political hobbles (on condition that it respect the rules of a modern and civilized "game," beginning with rules to protect the language and the dignity of its workers).

All these things, moreover, would open the door to a realization of Quebec's need to withdraw little by little, systematically, patiently, from its too exclusive dependence on American capital—a dependence which already is inevitably on the wane in any case. We must attract new partners, mainly European; here the S.G.F., Hydro, and *Soquem* have undertaken to do some prospecting which is beginning to bear modest fruit.

Finally, we don't dare say too much about planning, for too much already has been said, and too soon. . . . But in this new context we could well make a new start in this direction; this time, a serious start.

III WHAT ABOUT THE FLIGHT OF CAPITAL?

If we have a monetary union, the difficulties in this field can only be minimal.

Whatever happens, almost half our personal savings and half of the savings of the State of Quebec will continue to be channelled through the *Caisse de Dépôts* and the co-operative movement.

As for other financial institutions—insurance and trust companies, chartered banks, etc.—they naturally will be required to "incorporate" themselves in Quebec if they have not done so already. In this case they must, as is the general rule, build up or maintain in Quebec assets equivalent to the obligations or liabilities they will have contracted there.

It is, of course, possible that companies operating here may transfer their profits abroad. This happens, and always will happen, whatever the political system. The process will reach a level than can be termed that of serious "flight" only if conditions are unfavourable for the reinvestment of these mobile funds. Thus the only efficient solution, apart from emergency measures such as control of the movement of capital, is to create the best possible conditions. In no way does this require us to perform a collective act of licking the investors' boots, but rather we must pay strict attention to such things as better technical training among our workers, graduating professional people of ever-increasing competence, improving our transportation, and furnishing cheap, abundant power, etc.

Subject to these conditions, we would be justified in not worrying too much about individual lapses, for there always will be people who push the panic button, whatever happens!

Appendices

Appendix 1   Some Varieties of Special Status

There is a host of more or less valid definitions stating the basic minimum of powers and financial resources which Quebec must have.

These definitions can all be classed in the well-known category of "a special status in the strongest sense of the term." We maintain that it is impossible to achieve any of them within a federal framework, however the latter might be restructured.

This no doubt explains the unfortunate fact that the authors of such definitions extend them or trim them (depending on their monetary mood or the electoral atmospheric pressure), or go so far as to spread the various stages of such an achievement over one or even two generations!

But sometimes these authors get into print. . . . Here are a few such definitions, from among the most authoritative. First, a few quotations from the book which is Daniel Johnson's manifesto: *Equality or Independence*, published in 1965.

Before we decide on the form, let's decide on the content. . . .

The most important thing is to determine what powers are essential to an affirmation of the French-Canadian nation.

For nations as for individuals, there are fundamental liberties for which ones does not beg, and which cannot be the object of compromise or horse-trading.

The right of self-determination for the French-Canadian nation falls in this category. It is a collective patrimony which I consider to be ours, once and for all, and which I shall never consent to put up as a stake in any negotiation.

What we want is much more than those powers accorded to us in the constitution of 1867.

What we in fact want is the right to decide for ourselves, or to have an equal part in decision, in all areas that touch on our national life.

After all, are we really masters in our own house when Ottawa rules on everything concerning radio and television, media which in our age are perhaps the most effective arms of culture?

Are we masters in our own house when Ottawa refuses to give proper tariff protection to certain industries vital to French Canada?

Are we masters in our own house when Ottawa is in a position to use its immigration policies to modify the ethnic balance, to the point of putting us in a minority in the State of Quebec itself?

Are we masters in our own house when a decision made by the Bank of Canada can affect the credit of our businesses, our financial institutions, and even of the State of Quebec itself?

Are we masters in our own house when the federal treasury can skim off profits created by exploiting natural riches that belong to the community of Quebec, and, through the round-about means afforded by the corporation tax, prevent us from planning our economy in the way dictated by our peculiar need?

Are we masters in our own house when, through the inheritance tax, the federal government can upset the whole economy of our civil code?

Are we masters in our own house when nationalization is the only means left to us for the repatriation to Quebec of taxes imposed on our basic industries?

Are we masters in our own house when the Supreme Court, whose judges are all named by Ottawa, is the final interpreter of our French law and the only tribunal to which we can submit our grievances against the federal government?

These are a few of the ways in which Ottawa is able to interfere directly in our national life. These are some of the things that must be corrected if we want to enjoy self-determination as a nation. . . .

Federation, associate states, confederation, special status, republic—whatever form it takes, the new constitutional system must give the French-Canadian nation all the powers it needs to control its own destiny.

After three centuries of toil, our nation truly has earned the right to live freely. If we can feel at home from sea to sea, so much the better. This implies the recognition of our complete equality. If not, we shall be obliged to work for an independent Quebec.

Be it Canada or Quebec, wherever the French-Canadian nation can find liberty it also will find its homeland.

To this we must add at least a brief reminder of statements no less precise and no less public, made by other men of consequence who belong (or almost belong) to the present government of Quebec:

1 / For example, on June 30, 1967, Marcel Faribault advanced the following criticisms on the Constitution in a special issue of *Le Devoir* which has since been published in pocketbook form:*

Article 132 relative to treaties between the British Empire and foreign countries was intended to give parliament and the Canadian government all powers necessary or useful for the carrying out of Canada's obligations or those of any of its provinces, in the sense that these were a part of the Empire. Constitutional evolution has made this article totally inapplicable. . . .

The whole question of the nomination of Lieutenant Governors must be reviewed. . . .

Why must the judges of superior courts continue in our time to be named by the federal authority?

2 / Jean-Guy Cardinal, then Dean of the Faculty of Law at the University of Montreal and now Minister of Education, wrote in that same special issue:

We believe with Messrs. Faribault and Fowler, as they express it in Ten for One, *that the jurisdiction over savings banks contained in the British North America Act should be transferred to the provinces, which in effect means Quebec. In the same way the terms of a new constitution should transfer to the provinces jurisdiction over foundations and trust companies, insurance companies, co-operatives, caisses populaires, and other similar institutions. . . .*

Also in the special issue of June 30, 1967, the publisher of *Le Devoir*, Claude Ryan, gave a full description of the special status he proposes. Here are his more concrete suggestions:

1 / In the case of Quebec certain administrative transfers should be provided-for in a way that would make them possible without a constitutional amendment.

In this addition we are dealing with duplication of services and costs in areas such as employment agencies, agricultural

Le Québec dans le Canada de demain (Montreal: Edition du Jour, 1967).

credits, detention and rehabilitation of delinquents, and police forces. Without making an absolute principle of it, we fail to see why, in the case of Quebec, such services should not be carried out by the government of Quebec. Cultural and social reasons to justify such an arrangement are easy to see. And in the event of future constitutional reform, the possibility of such transfers should be provided for in the special case of Quebec. This was a grave omission in the Fulton-Favreau formula.

2 / In several areas of jurisdiction of a cultural and social nature, which in 1867 were not allocated to either level of government, it should be possible to provide at the same time for national schemes conceived and executed under normal Ottawa authority, and for the right of Quebec to assert a prior jurisdiction and to withdraw accordingly from such federal schemes, on condition that it received equal fiscal compensation. Among these areas we would particularly single out the following:

a / family allowances;
b / pensions and old-age pensions;
c / social welfare and assistance;
d / housing;
e / scholarships and students' allowances;
f / control of financial institutions, insurance and trust companies, commercial companies—except banks and other institutions which would remain for the most part under Ottawa;
g / regional and urban development;
h / scientific research in universities. . . .

3 / In international relations, broadcasting, and immigration, can we still honestly maintain, in 1967, that Ottawa's total and exclusive authority must be guarded as if under lock and key? If Quebec is in charge of governmental action in the realms of education and social security, if it has the primary responsibility for nurturing of the French Fact within its territory, how can we imagine that it should not have the right to extend its effectiveness through the establishment of international contracts which seem indispensable to the intelligent and complete exercise of its authority? How can we say that it should rely only on the Ottawa government to regulate and jealously control the functioning of radio and television within its territory, when that government goes so far as to refuse to Quebec the right to the slightest initiative in this field?

If Quebec has the primary responsibility for the development of French culture within its territory, how can we conceive that it should resign itself to allowing the federal government to exercise complete authority in the question of population? . . .

In certain cases there should be outright amendments to the British North America Act. Articles grown obsolete or ambiguous should be replaced by new provisions taking into account Quebec's special situation. In this connection, here are a few examples:

1 / Authority in question of marriage and divorce—subjects closely related to civil law and property—should be given outright to Quebec.

2 / The organization of the courts should be revised in such a way as to favour the development of more consistent civil rights and to provide clearer guarantees to Quebec in cases of final appeal, especially those of constitutional arbitration.

3 / The right of Quebec to have its own linguistic policy should be clearly established, as it is in other provinces. We do not mean by that to espouse indirectly a one-language policy in which we, personally, have little faith. We do intend hereby to protest most strongly against any constitutional text without clearer guarantees for Quebec.

4 / In the present wording of the B.N.A. Act, the central government has a number of very general powers, i.e., spending authority, the power to make laws for the peace, order, and good government of Canada, the power to decree that certain projects are of national interest, the power to assume authority in certain residual areas not mentioned in the constitution. Ottawa's interpretation of these powers repeatedly has given rise to deep discontent in Quebec. It was often the doorway through which the central power entered areas that should have been primarily the affair of the provinces, at least of Quebec. In a new constitution the content and exact limitations of these too-generous powers would have to be more rigidly defined. It should even be made quite clear that except for grave emergencies, such as a state of war or internal rebellion, Quebec should be quite free, whenever it chose, to dissociate itself from decisions made in Ottawa by virtue of such powers, without being financially penalized. In case of dispute, only a constitutional court duly accepted by all parties involved should have the authority to arbitrate.

5 / Finally, it would be essential to re-examine from top to bottom the make-up and role of the Canadian Senate, which scarcely answers the needs of a healthy federalism. . . .

a / It must be agreed that there is a limit to the proportion of direct taxation that Ottawa can cede to the provinces. According to certain experts this limit could vary from fifty to eighty per cent. In practice it could not reasonably to below thirty-five or forty per cent. . . .

There is, however, no reason to think that this proportion should be exactly the same for all provinces. It could remain at around forty per cent for the other provinces and rise somewhat more in Quebec's case, by reason of the exercise of jurisdiction in certain fields mentioned above. . . .

b / Apart from direct taxation, a considerable transfer of financial resources could also be made in the field of indirect taxes, especially under the federal sales tax and certain other taxes on tobacco and spirits. This idea has already been put forward several times by Robert Bourassa. It has been taken up recently by the Consultative Committee on Confederation formed by the Ontario government. In this connection it is useful to consult a study contained in the second volume of Background Papers and Reports *prepared by the Committee for Mr. Robarts' government. . . .*

Finally, from the Liberal side, we may reread to good advantage the following passages from the well-known report prepared for the party convention in October 1967 by Paul Gérin-Lajoie, then President of the Committee on Constitutional Affairs of the Quebec Liberal Federation:

The 1867 Constitution places a number of hindrances in the way of Quebec legislative action in areas which are, however, basic to ensure the permanence and development of Quebec's personality. . . .

We should note especially those loopholes in the Constitution through which the central government has made a side-door entry into areas elsewhere reserved exclusively for the provinces. Even if it means going into constitutional technicalities, we must mention here the wide reach of the clause on "peace, order, and good government," "residual" powers, "accessory" (or "incidental") authority, "proclamatory" powers, and, above all, the power to spend for any purpose whatever those revenues collected by virtue of an unlimited taxation authority. Under cover

*of this legal jargon are hidden not only direct but also more
insidious obstacles to the carrying-out of Quebec policies.*

The realms in which federal power has intruded in this way
vary from broadcasting to university subsidies, from welfare aid
and professional training to control of insurance and highway
construction. And what should we make of the too-subtle distinction between education and culture?

What more do we need to bring us to the conclusion that the
Constitution in its present form is a constant source of frustration and wasted energy, of duplication of function and conflict? If we are to have the smoothly functioning state that
Quebec requires, this situation must be changed radically. The
change necessarily involves a new division of powers. . . .

We can state that in one way every action — and thus every
power — of a state has a direct or indirect influence on the development of the collective personality of a people. But in an
age when the independence of nations is so much a part of
daily life that all states are seeking formulas for contact and co-
ordination, we must try to define what powers constitute the
minimum that can be ceded to an external authority without
endangering our individuality.

As soon as we speak of our collective personality, we evoke
everything which directly concerns language and culture: individual culture through educational institutions and the arts; mass
culture through films, radio, and television. These are areas
where Quebec must assume primary responsibilities and possess
the constitutional authority it needs to do so.

The development of this collective personality equally requires, too, that Quebec have an immigration policy that takes
into account its cultural and economic goals. For this purpose
Quebec must acquire more complete authority than that which
it has at the moment in this field, especially over the criteria of
selection and the actual selection of immigrants.

Social security and welfare, including health, are too directly
linked to the structure and values of society for Quebec not to
have exclusive responsibility for them. Political and administrative efficiency demand, moreover, that this sector be the responsibility of only one government.

The field of manpower, already related to two of the main
fields of jurisdiction of Quebec (education and labour), and involving special problems because of the language and culture
of Quebec labour, certainly can no more be left to outside

authority than can those of adult education and professional training.

The present and future responsibilities of the State of Quebec require it to have more extensive powers for the planning and development of its economy. The latter has such an influence on the states activity and the complete development of a collective personality and is, on the other hand, so conditioned by education, manpower and labour policies, social security, fiscal policy and public investment, that it is unthinkable for the State of Quebec not to have a role in affairs such as currency regulation, or credit and tariff policy. This does not imply that Quebec must have its own currency or establish its own customs service, but it must participate directly, of absolute necessity, in the creation of monetary and tariff policy. This is too important an instrument in the organization of our collective development for us to be excluded from it.

Jurisdiction over marriage and divorce, so closely related to the civil code, should be a Quebec prerogative. The same applies in the field of insurance, and commercial and financial companies, which are most important to our economic development.

In the modern world, if Quebec is to exercise its powers efficiently to ensure its maximum individual and collective development of its collectivity and its individuals, it must have complete sovereignty in those areas where it has exclusive prerogatives. This means that it should acquire a recognized international personality allowing it to negotiate agreements and to take part in international organizations whose activities coincide with the fields of Quebec's own sovereignty.

Finally, it is obvious that Quebec's sovereignty loses most of its meaning if the State of Quebec does not have the ability to modify its own constitution without restriction. This power should be clearly established. . . .

The above is a list that is neither complete nor definitive—far from it. We could add, for example, off-shore rights, maritime fisheries, certain categories of transportation, etc. . . . The State of Quebec must exercise this collection of powers in all sovereignty, with no limitations such as those now existing, which we have just outlined.

Above all, we must be well aware that the State of Quebec could not exercise these powers without a considerable increase in its financial resources. Within the hypothesis of a division of legislative jurisdictions between the State of Quebec and a central Canadian State, we must then provide, then, for a different fiscal division from that now in effect to correspond to the realignment of responsibilities.

The sovereignty of Quebec in this enlarged group of basic areas constitutes the extent of self-determination that seems from now on necessary to ensure the development of Quebec's collective personality. . . .

Then, looking for the best way to acquire this wide "fan" of sovereignty, Gérin-Lajoie comes to the point of espousing a special status which he places within a new federalism, involving:

The existence of a Central government and parliament directly elected by the people, with a life distinct from that of provinces or member-states and possessing powers defined by a constitution. This new federalism, with an original character proper to Canada, would provide that one of its member-states should enjoy a different status, distinct from that of the others. This different status would give Quebec full legislative and administrative powers in a number of fields which the other provinces could leave to the jurisdiction of the federal authority.

As we can see, these different "basic minimums" have a great deal in common. They all demand that Canada in fact accept a very new and extremely "original" kind of federalism. . . .

In effect the result would be a strange kind of arrangement where one would try to make *two* governments live together, each almost exactly as powerful and even as *central* as the other!

Such a project put forward by Quebec would deserve the slightly contemptuous smile that is reserved for those who want both liberty and a kind of all-risk insurance against liberty: *"to have your cake and eat it too."**

Appendix **2** Neo-centralization

On the "federalist" side, we find unequalled confusion.

Conventions of political engineers, closed retreats for "thinkers," the feverish patenting of *new Canadas*, succeed one an-

---

*In English in the original.

other at a rate which becomes faster and faster as we come closer we come to the inevitable moment of truth.

Among the many theses trying to breathe new life into "co-operative Federalism," and to push through with the help of this slogan the re-centralization that is the regime's only hope, let us glance at that put forward by Senator Maurice Lamontagne.

Of them all, this is certainly one of the best-expressed and most revealing. It is concise, clear, and for those who understand what they read, brutally frank.*

In short, all that Lamontagne offers us is the equality of the two "nations" *via* that old utopia: cultural duality.

This would be brought about by a series of more-or-less distant reforms which are noticeably (not to say strangely) reminiscent of those we are to find three months later in the Laurendeau-Dunton Report: creation of a bicultural Federal District and (gradual) "bilingualization" of the federal public service; (still gradual) extension of the French Network of the CBC; (again gradual) establishing of French schools for minorities comparable to those of the Anglo-Quebec population, and official "status" for the French language in Ontario and New Brunswick. . . .

Having "accomplished" all of that, sometime around the proverbial Thirtieth of February, Lamontagne goes from the unreal world to serious things to the only basic problem in the country: that of Quebec.

He attacks—and that is the exact expression for it—the argument for a special status. . . .

He chooses the framework proposed by the publisher of *Le Devoir*, Claude Ryan (see Appendix 1). He begins with a summary of it, after which he has the following comments, applied with merciless logic:

It would be easy to show that this kind of special status, with all its detailed implications, financial and other, leaves the federal government practically nothing to do in Quebec except turn over to the provincial government fiscal compensations financed in part by taxes collected in the rest of Canada. Even its economic role would become negligible. Why, then, not simply ask for the system of associate states? It would be much clearer, much more logical. Can it be for fear of the financial

---

*The passages we shall quote or paraphrase here appeared in *Le Devoir* on September 23 and 25, 1967.

consequences of such a system for Quebec? Or simply a general fear of what such an adventure could bring in its wake? I can see that for some it may seem advantageous to enjoy the status of an associate state while profiting from the protection that federalism affords.

As for Mr. Ryan, his position seems to be really one of negotiation, which consists of asking more at the start and accepting less at the end. In fact, before defining his concept of special status, he is careful to say to English Canada: "The first thing we ask of you is that you recognize with us the existence of the problems that arise out of the present constitutional confusion. We do not expect you to accept at once everything we propose to you. We expect, on the contrary, a tough and delicate bargaining process. We only ask that you recognize the facts from the start. . . ."

I, personally, favour the maintenance of a special status for Quebec within a true federalism, reformed according to the needs of our new society. This only conforms with reality. In my opinion the content of this special status can remain flexible and vary according to circumstances. What is more, those French-Canadians who believe in federalism must include in this special status only what they consider as clearly desirable for the well-being and development of the people of Quebec. We must, in short, make safe their way of life while protecting the standard of living and individual liberty.

The Federal State Renewed (And How)!

Over a Quebec that has been lulled back to sleep, nobly resigned to this "special *status quo*," Lamontagne can now lovingly sketch in the central state of his dreams.

His sketch is organized in six sections, admirably related to the "affluent society" and the dizzying scientific and technological revolution in which—as we also pointed out earlier—the main promises and dangers of our age await us.

After having demonstrated the great and fascinating law of change and even of perpetual motion, Senator Lamontagne shows how the modern state must learn increasingly how to provoke and stimulate this change, organizing it, helping its citizens to adapt to it and obtain the greatest benefits from it, but knowing how to circumvent it if necessary, and not forgetting the help the more highly developed peoples owe to others who also would like to see some changes. . . .

Then he has only to set up the agencies needed by the state to carry out these grandiose tasks. And, of course it, is to a "renewed" federal government that Lamontagne turns to fill this role in almost every case:

It is up to the federal government to assume the leading role in establishing scientific policy. To this end it should double its efforts in the course of the coming years and carry out a radical transformation of its administrative structures. It should create a federal department of scientific affairs, as several countries already have done, broken down into three institutions which would deal respectively with the physical sciences, the sciences of life, and the human sciences. To these would be added the Science Council of Canada and the Scientific Secretariat. Such a department would centralize the efforts now being made by several federal services and in particular would replace the Department of Energy, Mines, and Resources as now constituted. . . .

We also should not prevent the central government from planning within the limits of its jurisdiction. We should, therefore, create at the federal level a Department of Planning which would replace that of the Treasury Board. As for the Economic Council of Canada, it should be prevented from becoming a permanent Royal Commission on economic problems, and be reformed so as to be in a better position to provide guide-lines for the private sector. . . .

It is understood that education at all levels should continue to be the affair of the provinces. However, beyond the field of education in the strict and traditional sense of the word—the "formal" sense, as one says in English—the federal government can dissociate itself from various aspects of manpower policy, simply because of its responsibilities in economic growth, adaptation to technological change, and unemployment. This is why the federal Minister of Manpower and Immigration must continue his efforts to eliminate what economists call the "friction" which may exist in the labour market and promote mobility of manpower to the greatest possible degree. . . .

A Department of Welfare and Labour should combine those of Health and Welfare, the Registrar General, and Labour. Its responsibility would be to administer purely federal aspects of social security, ensure the protection of the consumer and the solution of labour conflicts within federal jurisdiction, and, finally, carry out the federal function in urban reform. Elsewhere, a Department of Regional Development should replace that of Rural Development, co-ordinate the federal struggle against poverty at the regional level, and take charge of the Area Development Agency now under the Department of Industry. The latter should disappear, and any of its responsibilities not taken over by the Departments of Regional Development and Scientific Affairs could be given to the Department of Commerce. . . .

The central government, given its constitutional responsibilities, should have a cultural policy, and should attach a higher importance to it in times of affluence. Since 1964, the different federal cultural institutions have been grouped under a single departmental "roof"—that of the Secretary of State. This should now become in name what it is in fact a Department of Cultural Affairs. . . .

By continuing to exercise its traditional functions, with which we have not dealt here, and by putting the accent on the role it should play in an era of plenty, the federal government would remain strong and flexible enough to balance the new power of the provinces. With leadership and structure reflecting the new priorities in its responsibilities, it would be in a position to perform its task more efficiently within, of course, a system of co-operative federalism.

It is in his conclusion that Lamontagne is guilty of his only piece of false naïveté. In fact, when he says he has in mind only that Ottawa should "balance" the power of the province, he is gently pulling our leg. . . .

For, if we think for a moment, we realize that his projects would in fact ensure, in fact, the existence of an all-powerful federal state and a new start on the old path to centralism, the State of Quebec quickly and forever becoming that "oversized municipal council" that was Sir John A. Macdonald's dream.

With small alterations here and there, this is what all our more lucid "thinkers" or agents of "co-operative federalism" are proposing.

They see as clearly as Jacques Parizeau (see Appendix 3) the continuous movement toward the decrease of federal power. In this emergency the only solution from their point of view is a radical reinforcement of that power for they are unable to conceive of living in a world from which it had been subtracted. If they want to succeed, they are totally obliged to "put down"

Quebec once and for all, before it is too late. And so in desperation they administer the anaesthetic of cultural duality from sea to sea, in the hope unconsciousness will last until the operation has been completed painlessly.

Appendix **3** Quebec–Canada: A Blind Alley

DECENTRALIZATION — BALKANIZATION

In this section you will find, almost *in extenso,* one of the most penetrating analyses ever made of the Canada-Quebec crisis.

Originally, it was a speech at Banff on October 17, 1967, to a major convention of economic experts. The English-language press, among them the *Financial Post* and the *Financial Times,* at once saw the implications immediately and devoted considerable space to their comments on it.

In Quebec, we had to wait until mid-November (apart from some brief, well-buried mentions) for *Le Devoir*–who else but *Le Devoir?*–to inform the public of the speech in an adequate way.

The author's competence alone and the importance of the role he has played for some years should really have brought the text more attention than this. . . . He returned late in 1967 to a teaching post at *l'Ecole des Hautes Études Commerciales.* Professor Parizeau is a graduate of the H.E.C., holds a degree from the *Institut d'Études Politiques* in Paris, and a Ph.D. in Economics from the London School of Economics. After being in charge of research for the (Porter) Royal Commission on banking and finance, and acting as a member of the teams which did the preparatory work for the nationalization of electric power and later the *Régime des Rentes* and the *Caisse des Dépôts* (Quebec's Pension Board and Fund), he was director of research for the Quebec delegation on the Federal-Provincial Tax Committee on Fiscal Regulations (1964-66) and chairman of the Committee of Enquiry into Quebec's financial institutions, which completed its work toward the end of 1967. Most important, he was economic and financial adviser to the Quebec cabinet from 1965 to 1967. He is thirty-seven years old.

I

Parizeau begins by attempting to go straight to get to the heart of the idea of decentralization, "which implies a concept of orientation but with no precise content." After identifying the two forms of decentralization (administrative and political) and distinguishing in the second form between the kind where a central authority continues to establish priorities and that in which it loses the power to do so, he describes the dangers to a country's efficiency and to its very equilibrium under excessive decentralization of the command mechanism. He goes on:

Thus, the conclusion is inescapable. Proper economic policies can be achieved or even can be helped through administrative decentralization. They can still be worked out properly according to the first formula of policy decentralization, whereas given programs are adapted to local and regional differences. But as soon as the central policy-making apparatus loses control over priorities and a common if not identical level of public services, the broad objectives of an efficient economic policy are put in jeopardy.

There is nothing particularly new in such a conclusion.

Western industrialized countries have been built during the nineteenth and early twentieth centuries, on the basis of growing centralization both of policy and administration. In recent years administrative decentralization has set in usually because central agencies were getting to be so large as to be unmanageable. Furthermore, the abuses implicit in global policies inherited from the Keynesian theoretical stream have been so noticeable, particularly in the neglect of regional discrepancies of growth and income level, that some margin of autonomy at the policy level has been given to regional authorities, although experiments in that direction are still inconclusive. Few countries, however, have agreed to go much further, except if historical and political reasons forced them to do so.

"How Does Canada Fit into This Pattern?"

The B.N.A. Act gave to provinces complete powers to determine their own priorities in important fields of activity, complete powers to raise certain taxes to the level they wished, and, most surprisingly, unlimited powers to borrow at home and abroad.

By any standards, this political structure should have pro-

duced appalling economic policies. No doubt, it did produce some pretty bad ones from time to time, but as we all know when social and economic policies of the Keynesian era had to be set up, they were actually saved by the War. With low financial resources, provinces could have only a limited sphere of influence on such decisions while the central government was in a financial position to carry through the required policies and have the constitution amended when necessary. Thus the end result was not as bad as could have been feared, and to all practical purposes Canada got equipped with all the trappings of modern economic and social economic policies just as quickly and efficiently as if it had been a unitary state.

As pressures on provinces became greater because of the needs of education, road, transport, urban renewal, a shift of resources started from the federal government to the province that took, as we all know, three distinct forms: first, shared-cost program transfers; second, unconditional abatement in tax fields previously occupied by the federal government; and third, equalization.

Shared-cost programs afford one of the best examples of the muddle in concepts that has emerged with respect to government planning and policy-making. Essentially, the technique was an excellent one that offered the federal government the possibility of establishing priorities and then making sure that they would be carried out, as they had to be respected by provinces if money was to be paid out to them. Of course the techniques that evolved from the original idea were often abusive and wasteful. When every book bought by a technical school had to be individually approved by Ottawa, or when lighting fixtures of hospital corridors created crisis between governments, it became obvious that attempts at centralization had reached the limits of ridicule.

Yet the idea behind the shared-cost program was the proper one. The central policy-making agency had the required instrument to keep priorities throughout the country in line with what the main social values of the time seemed to require.

It would have been relatively easy to decentralize the administration, leave some margin of decision to the provinces, as indeed was done occasionally. It would also have been easy to incorporate into shared-cost programs a wide measure of equalization. . . .

If this had happened, we would probably be discussing

today of the amount of freedom that provinces should have in tailoring construction standards according to local conditions or in shifting money from one local project to another. Voices would be heard in favour of bloc grants. And surely objections would certainly be forthcoming to having the Auditor General recheck operations that have already been examined by the provincial auditors. Futhermore, the federal government would have to yield somewhat to the pressures exercised by provincial premiers to the effect that priorities should not be changed into immediate objectives before prior consultations.

In other words, we would be discussing decentralization and co-operation in the context of what one may call a normal country where economic and social policy is by and large the result of a consensus and is organized as such. Provinces would indeed have some resources that they could channel according to their own objectives. But both with respect to the size of the amounts involved and to the type of expenditures into which this money could flow, there would be few risks that the national objectives and programs be jeopardized or even appreciably hindered.

We, actually, came very close to achieving such a result. However, when we now talk of decentralization we refer really to a process that has little in common with what I have just stressed as a sort of ideal. How did we miss and how did the present situation arise any way?

Development in Recent Years: Chaotic Rather Than Rational Decentralization

The shift of resources to the provinces has largely been unconditional. Thanks to such a shift some provincial governments have been in a position to embark upon projects of their own and have in recent years improved to a remarkable extent their administrative and policy-making staff. In other words, they have tended to become once again real governments. It would of course be an exageration to assume that all provinces were in a position to follow such a course, but some obviously did. Let us consider, for instance, the remarkable change that occured in Ontario between the time when its government started co-operating so closely with the federal government in the financing of a first-class network of technical and vocational schools, and the statement of less than two years ago in which it states unequivocally that regional development inside its borders falls predominantly within its jurisdiction.

In parallel, the federal government became more and more reluctant to push forward with shared-cost programs. One province had negotiated its opting out from several of these. The next step war for the central government to offer its own withdrawal from some major programs in the field of social security. Medicare was then offered as a mitigated form of shared-cost program.

The last step was taken a year ago, when the abatement system that had ruled for years the sharing of direct taxes between governments was cancelled. This step had considerable significance in a symbolic sort of way. Until then the federal government had in a sense limited the access of provinces to additional fiscal resources in the field of direct taxes. Without its approval, provinces were not likely to embark on their own into a raise of tax rates. Indeed, they still could get additional resources by shifting their indirect tax schedules, so that effective control by the central government was a partial one. But partial as it was, it vanished.

From now on, each government will be in a position to tax as it sees fit.

With respect to public debt, provinces had never been subject to federal control, but at least they were subject to some sort of market discipline. A limit did exist with respect to the amounts that could be borrowed. That limit was raised with the introduction of the Canada Pension Plan, whereas the federal government agreed to shift all the yield of contributions to provinces, without any indication or limitation as how that money was to be spent. Such loans did not, of course, reduce the market borrowing of provinces; in fact, it went on rising. Again the transfer of C.P.P. funds to provinces was to all practical purposes an unconditional transfer.

Evidently the collapse of central policy-making can be called decentralization of a fashion.

It has also implied under the impetus of unconnected spending programs, an uncontrolled increase of public expenditures and a pressure on the economy that may have medicare as its first victim. Unchecked, unconnected, spending programs of all governments have used up available resources and more.

What happens to priorities? This question has been asked

repeatedly by some politicians at all government levels. The answer is not forthcoming. Nobody really knows. In fact, what is a priority now? Some objective over which a federal-provincial conference has agreed to? But what have been the objectives over which such an agreement has taken place in the recent past? Medicare is one, but it is already obvious that what looked like an agreement, is not an agreement any more.

I know that some analysts are not as pessimistic as I am. The ability of the central government to pursue effective stabilization policies would, according to them, not have been seriously impaired by what has happened. The federal government would still be in a position to conduct major growth policies, in addition to what provinces have embarked upon.

All this is correct up to a point. Yet an efficient economic policy cannot exist if part of the public sector operates without much reference to what the other part is doing, and surely a government is not doing a proper job if it is not in a position to control the total level of taxes, public expenditures, and the public debt. Economics, said Lawrence Klein, is commonsense, and economic theory is commonsense made difficult. No matter how refined our explanations and discussions, commonsense cannot be neglected for very long.

Be that as it may, we have now reached a point where we want to translate, into constitutional changes, shifts toward the decentralization of economic and social policy that I suggest have in any case gone much too far. If we were to consolidate in constitutional terms the present situation, it is very doubtful indeed whether any rational planning within Canada would ever become possible. A country should not be allowed to balkanize decision-making to the extent that exists now, and even more so to the extent that are more and more often suggested by so many constitution builders.

Quebec: A Unique Case

The trouble comes from Quebec, and from nowhere else. We try to discuss in general or even in abstract terms of economic and social powers, of the merits of a decentralized society, of avant-garde *techniques of public administration, while all the time we know full well that hardly any ripple would be raised in such respects if Quebec did not exist or else if it agreed to fall in the mainstream.*

Every step toward unconditional shifts of resources to prov-

inces originated in a crisis with Quebec. Ever since Duplessis ordered double taxation in 1954, and thus forced the federal government of the day to yield a part of the income tax field it occupied, one crisis after another led to further shifts.

From one year to the next, the federal government offered new shifts of resources of a conditional nature. Time after time successive Quebec governments managed to get the conditions loosened, to get transition periods established after which conditions would vanish, to obtain fiscal equivalences and so on. When Quebec retired from twenty-nine shared-cost programs, the conditions were so confused for a while as to what would happen at the end of the transition period that the federal Prime Minister and the Quebec Premier managed to contradict each other officially, in the best of faith on both sides.

With respect to the Pension Plan program, an agreement was worked out, but the Quebec pension plan and the Canada pension plan are completely distinct, and the investment policies that are derived from their operation have nothing in common.

At the end of 1965, Premier Lesage flatly stated that, from then on, Quebec would not accept conditional grants any more. Whether he was believed or not is immaterial. The fact remains that federal payments for post-secondary education were tailored in such a way that they could be used by provincial governments for roads or public works if they so wished. Truly, these payments were unconditional.

In other words, the policy followed by Quebec government has been largely consistent over a long stretch of years; more and more money or taxation powers with no strings attached. They did not want decentralization of policies, they wanted to follow their own policies.

Every abuse of the shared-cost program approach, every inconsistency, every failure, was used by Quebec to discredit the formula. Whenever shared-cost programs provided a given amount of money for capital expenditures, Quebec drained sooner or later whatever was available. New current programs? The answer was always no, or methods were found to stop the suggestion even before it was officially made.

The results have been rather startling on the attitude of other provinces. Some thought that they could handle far more of the administration than the several programs provided for. As governments, they wanted to be treated as such, and possibly

Ottawa was too late to recognize it. Other governments were worried with the priorities that too often the federal government established without prior consultations.

For one reason or another, Quebec mustered unexpected support on numerous occasions, and that support, in times of crisis, was often invaluable. . . .

Indeed, the federal government did try, as was mentioned previously, to opt itself out of a number of existing social-security programs. Provinces were not interested. In fact, politicians and officials from provinces outside Quebec did not really understand what substance there was in such a move except as a curious way of trying to bring them in line with Quebec.

II THE HEART OF THE MATTER

The heart of the matter is that provinces by and large are not at all ready to consider any drastic changes in the federation to which they belong. Individual provinces have conflicts from time to time with the federal authorities, such as in the case of off-shore mineral rights or securities legislation; they may be hard-pressed from time to time by financial difficulties, and if Federal leadership is not forthcoming, some of them, but by no means all, will operate on their own and develop new programs.

But by and large there are no serious reasons why nine provinces out of ten would not within the present constitutional framework accept readily, even eagerly, and in some cases with relief, strong central leadership with decentralization being limited to administrative procedures and what I have called the first formula of policy determination. There are indeed historical and political differences of some magnitude between provinces. Emotions are pinned to local or regional characteristics and are not likely to vanish quickly. Yet, these provinces actually belong to a country in more senses than just sharing a common citizenship. Deep differences with regard to social values are not very numerous, and those that exist are, as they should be, more readily reflected by political parties than by provincial or local administrations.

It does not, however, follow from all this that a constitutional revision would be a fruitless exercise for English-speaking provinces. A great deal must in fact be done to the present con-

stitution to improve its workability. In several fields the old wording is hopelessly out of date. Distinctions between education, training, and culture must be drawn to cut short too many discussions. Everything connected with incorporation of companies, the control over financial institutions, and securities legislation must be dealt with afresh so that at last governments can easily determine who does what. Similarly, we should get rid of the absurd distinction between direct and indirect taxes that may have had some sense for lawyers slightly exposed to the writings of John Stuart Mill, but does not make any sense at all in our days.

It is remarkable, however, that such changes do not imply necessarily a further process of decentralization. They are necessary to clarify the present situation but certainly not be bolster provincial action. They are needed to avoid gaps and overlapping that has been noticeable for a long time.

Indeed, swaps of powers or jurisdiction can even be contemplated to improve the efficiency of the system. The periodic interventions of the federal government at the local level has not always had the best of results. When it comes to dealing with municipalities, the confrontation of provincial and federal initiatives or administration has often been a source of waste and, in a way, of blackmail, with municipalities sitting pretty between competing government agencies. Still, it is a most extraordinary feature of our federation, that, while the federal government is responsible for the balance of payments, monetary policy, and in general stabilization policies, provincial governments have an unlimited power to borrow abroad as well as domestically.

Surely a case could be made whereas provinces would not have to be competing with Ottawa for municipal gratitude, just as a case could be made for the federal government to be in a position to supervise provincial borrowing particularly on foreign markets, whenever the economic situation of the country warrants it.

Finally it may be possible to include in the Constitution provisions for consultative machinery. I, personally, am not sure that the best way to improve present consultation is to include mandatory provisions or relevant organizations into a Constitution, but if such measures can alleviate fears, why should it not be done?

Be that as it may, a revision of the Constitution may well be needed to help the workings of our political and economic system. As indicated above, it is not as complex a job as is often feared, and it could go a long way in bringing the B.N.A. *Act up to date.*

The Quebec Government, Spokesman for a Society that Will Continue to Emphasize Its "Difference"

All governments involved have enough experience in such technical matters to proceed rapidly. Yet the stumbling-block is again Quebec.

What does Quebec want?

Nobody knows for certain. A continuing process has set in. With little influence or weight in Ottawa for a very long time, French Canadians turned more and more to the Quebec government in the late fifties and early sixties. It was not much of a government. It had traditionally been inefficient and corrupt. But it was there and could be used. It was slowly reactivated. There lay the possible expression of social values that had never truly recognized at the federal level. A society cannot live for long without a government, and French Canadians either had none or were ashamed of the one they had had. They flexed their muscles and were surprised by the early results. They were not sure of their technical ability, and came out of their first technical confrontation with the rest of the country without ridicule.

The nationalization of Hydro-Electric companies, the General Investment Corporation, the Caisse de Dépôt et Placement, Soquem, *the* Société de Crédit Industriel, *the school revolution, the Quebec Pension Plan, new family allowances, Sidbec, the general increase of taxation powers, a wage policy in the public sector—these were so many examples of an exciting discovery. French Canadians in Quebec could set themselves concrete objectives, achieve them fully, partially, or even fail to meet them, like any other people. To consider that all of this is oriented toward the well-being of the élite or the bourgeois is sheer humbug. The enormous increase in secondary schooling, the doubling of the minimum wage level in three years, a status of union bargaining in the public sector that is now unique in North America—these are not measures that ar really bourgeois oriented.*

There Will Be No Stopping Quebec's Self-Affirmation

The fact is that the so-called quiet revolution has had deep roots in all of French-Canadian society and is now quite irreversible. It can be slowed down, but one does not really see how it could be stopped. No one knows at any rate where it will stop. The discovery that existing values can be reflected in political decisions brings people to crystallize vague ideas into real values. For governments, experiments become feasible and in some cases politically rewarding.

In other words what has happened in Quebec City over the last few years is the emergence of government process in a society that is fairly homogeneous and which does not necessarily have the same objective as the rest of the country. Let me be more specific about this with at least one example. Social security for the old has been immensely improved in Canada recently. In Quebec, it is now understood by an increasing number of people that the combination of a rapidly declining birth rate and the failure to assimilate immigrants into the French stream present dreadful dangers for the French community in North America. The reorganization of family allowances, facilities for working mothers, and new immigration policies became objectives of far greater significance than in the rest of the country, at the expense no doubt of old-age pensions, an issue that in any case was never as acute in Quebec as in the rest of the country, in part due to the fact that, as a proportion of the population, there are fewer old people in Quebec than in the rest of Canada.

I know that some elected members of Quebec ridings in Ottawa tend to play down the differences. Some politicians in Quebec City emphasize them for bargaining purposes. No doubt it is so difficult to know what Quebec wants. What I suggest, however, is that Quebec will probably want more and more, that the development of government process in the provincial capital will not be reversed in the years to come. I also submit that the failure of the federal government to be, for such a long time, a French-Canadian as well as English-Canadian government, is in part responsible for the vacuum that was created. Indeed, efforts are now made in Ottawa to correct the situation. It may well be too late. When a society has been for so long in search of fulfillment and has found it within itself, it is very unlikely that it can be distracted from this purpose.

The Worst Mistake: Trying To Make Quebec Into "Just Another Province"

Sure, it is possible to discredit a given government in Quebec, to stall it, to undermine its authority. It is even possible for such a government to abdicate. But the historical process is to my mind quite inevitable.

How then do we reconcile the requirements of economic policy with such a political disturbance? The answer, of course, is that we don't. We should not even try.

Attempts to deal with all provinces of Canada in the same way, when it comes to economic, financial, or social policies is about the worse of all possible courses. It will for most of Canada imply a degree of decentralization that is wasteful and, on the long run, dangerous. At the same time such a course will necessarily fall short sooner or later of what Quebec governments want, no matter how generous it might have seem at the outset.

The answer lies in recognizing that we are faced with two different societies, that efficient economic policies for one are not necessarily efficient economic policies for the other because values are different, that there is no need to sacrifice efficiency for the larger society to accommodate the smaller one, which is likely in any case to be dissatisfied with the compromise.

Whether Quebec will, or will not, have a special status is a byzantine question. It already has one over a wide spectrum of activities. It will get more sooner or later. It might even become independent. What is important in the meantime is that the economics of all of Canada not be sacrificed to political skirmishing. What we should really be looking for now are ways to co-ordinate the policies that will arise from these two societies so that not too much economic and social harm will arise while the awakening of Quebec takes place.

Appendix **4** The Snare of Biculturalism

At the end of 1967 came "Operation Panic."

We were given stronger doses than ever of that good old soporific: the French fact *from coast to coast.**

*Cf. the text by Father Richard Arès below. In English in original.

At the end of November came the Confederation of To-morrow Conference; then, early in December, publication of Volume One of the "B. and B." report.

In the first of these, Quebec was to encounter a stone wall so far as "special status" was concerned (see Appendix 1). The extension of the powers and financial resources of our national state—the only basic question—was simply juggled out of sight.

Still, the politicians meeting in Toronto privately passed the good word along on the subject of French minorities. Even Ernest Manning, absolutely intransigent until then, became quite touching in his final remarks on the subject. . . . And Daniel Johnson was able to back down to a position of bicultural good fellowship: "I've laid a kind of bet on the future of Canada in a new federalism based on cultural duality. . . .*

There is a flexibility here that allows for the political meandering contained in the famous slogan of "Equality or Independence." This completely ambiguous phrase can in fact be interpreted—according to the needs of the moment!—either in the political sense (equality for Quebec, a distinct national society) or in the cultural sense (equality of the two "founding peoples" building a do-it-yourself bi-country from St. John's to Victoria!).

Since the Toronto conference Messrs. Johnson, Marcel Fari-bault, and Co. seem to have decided on the second version, which they evoke without stopping for a breath.

. . . As if by chance, it was no more than a few days after that conference that the first massive tome of the report of the Royal Commission on Bilingualism and Biculturalism appeared. In it we encounter the principal recommendations for reform already voiced so many times by the most prominent Quebec "federalists" (see Appendix 2).

The outstanding addition to these is the concept of "bilingual districts." Based on census breakdowns, these would be set up (or perhaps dismantled!) following federal-provincial negotiations after each decennial head-count.

As such districts would for the most part be concentrated in the three adjacent provinces of Ontario, Quebec, and New Brunswick, it is here that the report is most insistent: the B. and B. Commission proposes that Ontario, and New Brunswick proclaim themselves to be officially bilingual without delay, following the example imposed in former days upon Quebec.

*Daniel Johnson, quoted in *Le Devoir*, December 1, 1967.

A hundred years ago this might have been. . . . But we'll never know for sure!

And even twenty-five years ago Quebec perhaps would have found in such a move the pretext for settling down to another eternity of patience and delusion.

But today this slow-motion idealism enters the race like a utopian tortoise trudging along after the hare of galloping assimilation. But unlike the hare in the fable, this one is already winning. . . .

I "DO WE DROP OUR PREY TO CATCH ITS SHADOW?"

This latest announcement of the creation of the kind of country we have been denied for the last hundred years is yet another attempt to anaesthesize Quebec public opinion which finally is dangerously awake to its own interests.

If the anaesthetic should "take," the emergency would be over for a long, long time. In fact, how many generations would be required (for we must be reasonable, mustn't we?) to see transformed into a binational bicultural environment those nine provinces which have never been anything but an English-speaking melting-pot? Another hundred years? That's certainly what they hope. . . .

Thus, instead of strengthening Quebec, they talk of a revival of French-Canada outside our borders.

Let us say it very, very calmly: what they are proposing to us now is a sucker's game.

First, we must first note the advanced stage of cultural decay of our minorities in the other provinces. The table I have printed below is taken from the only serious studies made, to my knowledge, about this aspect of the 1961 census: those of the Rev. Richard Arès, s.J., in the March 1963 and May 1964 issues of the review *Relations*.

Take a good look at the frightening speed of assimilation. More than a third of the members of our minority groups already declared themselves as English-speaking six years ago. In fact, some thirty-four per cent speak *only English*.

Father Arès, on checking other censuses since 1931, also found that the process of assimilation has accelerated constantly. One is forced to believe that since 1961 the situation has continued to deteriorate.

Was this not indicated with brutal clarity in a poll pub-

GALLOPING ASSIMILATION
Census of 1961

	Of French "Origin"	French Still "Mother Tongue"	Assimi-lated	Per Cent Assimi-lated
N.B.	232,127	210,530	21,597	9.3
MAN.	83,986	60,899	23,037	27.4
ONT.	647,941	425,302	222,639	34.3
SASK.	59,824	36,163	23,661	39.5
YUKON and N.W.T.			966	40.0
ALTA.	83,319	42,276	41,043	49.2
P.E.I.	17,418	7,958	9,460	54.3
N.S.	87,883	39,568	48,315	54.9
B.C.	66,970	26,179	40,791	60.8
NFLD.	17,171	3,150	14,021	81.6
TOTAL	1,296,589	852,025	445,530	34.3

lished by *Le Devoir* some months ago? If my memory serves me right, we read there of a multitude of "ordinary" New Brunswick Acadians, far removed from the fragile surviving élite, who were almost completely indifferent to "superfluous" questions such as French schools and French television.

Now, New Brunswick's French-speaking population has suffered far less from official encroachments than any of our other provincial minorities. The Acadians, in all the glory of their legendary sufferings, are not very far from attaining the magic figure of fifty per cent of the province's population. And yet, behind this fine façade. . . .

Nowhere else, in any case, not even in Ontario where the numbers as such seem impressive, does the French-speaking population reach eight per cent of the total.

And above all, nowhere can they count on a tenth of the advantages given to our eighteen per cent English-speaking population so that they could consolidate their position here in Quebec.

Minorities: "In Quebec, conquerors . . . elsewhere, immigrants"

We must not forget that the ancestors of the English-speaking minority in Quebec came here as conquerors. It was perfectly natural for them to grab the real power which economic domination gives. This allowed them not only to build themselves high schools well before we had our *secondaires* and McGill before Laval, but also to grant themselves exorbitant privileges such as the traditional saw-off of the "neutral" tax in Montreal.*

They have been enabled to build a powerful press in the *Gazette* and the *Star* and obtained with no trouble at all Channels 6 and 12 in television and a quaintly excessive number of radio stations. . . .

In the rest of Canada, our French-speaking minorities arrived poor and timid and have been treated like any group of foreign immigrants.

Day labourers, miners, or lumberjacks for Northern Ontario, "displaced" farmers in the Prairies, a battalion of *cheap labour*† recruited for the sawmills of the Fraser and how transformed into "Maillardville," B.C.

Even today they are not exactly economic winners—while the Quebec English constitute, by and large, *the richest group in the whole country*.

Sucked into the melting-pot, condemned like other new arrivals of every origin to anglicize themselves for survival, our minorities were natural candidates for assimilation. This is the price of climbing the socio-economic ladder.

The fact is, indeed, that the best "preserved" are usually the most isolated, the poorest, the worst-educated. These are also the ones with the least understanding of Quebec today. These people, who left for faraway places in 1910 or 1930, have retained memories of *la belle province* as it was in those days— memories as exact and touching as they are exasperating. When they talk about present problems, you would think you were listening to the scarcely audible echo of an old speech by Bourassa. . . .

A good number of professional people who have survived, among them those who had such difficulty putting up with the atmosphere of the Estates-General, have built their careers, in all sincerity, by preserving this archaic outlook.‡

*For school taxation purposes, there are three valuation rolls in Quebec: Roman Catholic; Protestant, including Jews; and Neutral, for corporations.
†In English in the original.
‡Those who have taken such a close look at how "representative" the Estates-General meeting was from the point of view of Quebec

"The Great Delusion"

And now, how can they improve their lot?

By obtaining (as so many honestly believe and others less naively maintain) advantages comparable to those our English-speaking Quebeckers enjoy?

First on the list would be the urgent need for equally good schools, from primary to university level—for relatively poor minorities which are often highly dispersed and, except in New Brunswick, do not add up to even half the percentage formed by English-speaking minority in Quebec!

And what would be the result of this most improbable effort? It would throw into a labour market and social climate—completely English in character, a host of people trained and competent to work within a French culture! Or, more likely, it would repatriate them to Quebec as they became prepared (something gained, at least!).

Finally, how is this to happen in a country where at the slightest sign of an economic slowdown the first cuts are made in those services that are the most essential? And at a time when the pressing needs of the *present* educational system are calculated in hundreds of millions of additional dollars? A wonderful dream—and a sad joke! Trying to sell us such a Utopia would be as fraudulent as the eternal promise made to the Negroes by American segregationists of a school system that would be "separate but equal," a system they will no more see in the future than they have in the past. . . .

To sum up, they would like to substitute for our objective (which is the essential emancipation of Quebec) only a pale shadow, a pious impossibility.

might well take equal pains to see if the delegates of minorities outside Quebec were themselves representative. . . . However that may be, as early as his inaugural address on November 23, 1967, the President, Jacques-Yvan Morin, foresaw these divergent "wavelengths" which the voting was to reveal: "We saw very clearly in the game that the questions which interest Quebec and those which outside groups are not the same. While the Acadians or the French Canadians from Ontario or the West put the emphasis on their collective rights, such as language and education, Quebec delegates talk about areas of jurisdiction and governmental powers. There is no point in going into the historical causes of this difference in approach to the national problem, but it is most important that all delegates accept from the start these tendencies dictated by the nature of things."

"This would be a race against the clock and against the stream. It is an interminable, depressing race, lost before the start." (René Lévesque, December 3, 1967)

II "WHAT KIND OF EQUALITY?
FOR WHOM AND BY WHOM?"

The debate on the political future of Quebec goes on with growing intensity. Little by little it is invading all the information media, the pressure and special interest groups, the political parties, and almost every level of the populace of Quebec. After General de Gaulle's visit and René Lévesque's public stand, no political party can afford to ignore it or refuse to take part in it, even if for some it seems to be a waste of time in futile discussion, a "collective obsession."

Among the many slogans to which this debate has given birth one of the most popular beyond a doubt is that launched by the leader of the Union Nationale: Equality or Independence! At first sight, nothing seems clearer than such a slogan: either French Canadians are given equality or they declare themselves independent. Their first and principal demand is for equality; as for independence, it takes second place and is seen as a kind of Damocles' sword suspended over the head of English Canada to make it consent to the sacrifices required by equality. The key word of the slogan thus is equality. But what kind of equality are we talking about? Equality with whom? For whom? But whom? As we look a little more deeply into this well-known slogan, we discover that it opposes a clear notion, that of independence, to a clouded notion, a notion that seems falsely clear: that of equality.

The great virtue of the idea of independence is that it can be seen in a form which everyone can understand, that it defines clearly and totally the scope of the alternative. No one can be in doubt: the independence we are talking about is that *of* Quebec, *for* Quebec, and *by* Quebec. Those who advocate it are more and more abandoning expressions like "French-Canadian nation," "French Canada," "French Canadians," and replacing them by "Quebec nation," "Quebec," and "*Québécois.*" Does not René Lévesque's manifesto begin with these words: "We are *Québécois!*" It follows that independence is not for the French-Canadian nation as a whole, but for the French minorities in the other provinces; it is for the *Québécois,* and first and foremost for the *Franco-Québécois*. In the same way it is *by* the *Franco-Québécois*: they are the ones who feel the need and lead the struggle for it. . . .

It would be gratifying if the idea of equality had the same clarity as that of independence. Unfortunately, this is not the case. One of the most striking proofs is the fact that every political party has more or less agreed with the objective of achieving equality. Even the federal parties go so far as to repeat in chorus, "Equality yes, independence, no!" As for partisans of independence, they can be found even within the present federal system. If parties with such conflicting convictions can agree so easily to use the same word, is it not a sign that they are not all using it in the same sense nor attributing to it the same meaning?

Equality for Whom?

Equality for whom? The reply may at first glance seem simple and clear: for French-Canadians. But who are the French-Canadians? When we look closely at the situation in Canada today, we discover that there are at least three ways of considering it, and that in each case equality is involved: French-Canadians as individuals; as a national community; and as a political society.

For some, there are simply individuals of French origin in Canada, just as there are individuals of German, Ukrainian, or Jewish origin. To these individuals they are ready to grant equality before the law, an equality guaranteed by a proclamation or a bill of rights. To the demands of French Canadians, they like to reply, "Well, what are you complaining about? You have the same rights and freedoms as other citizens: why do you keep demanding privileges that we can give you only if we also give them to members of other ethnic groups?"

This purely legalistic and individual equality is one that everybody is willing to guarantee to French Canadians. But can the latter be satisfied with it? The answer, of course, is no. French Canadians are more than a collection of individuals: they form a national community with its own culture and history, and today they prefer to call themselves a nation. The problem of equality thus can never be satisfactory solved in Canada unless we agree to go beyond the individual level and consider it frankly on a collective basis.

French Canadians, I repeat, form a national community, but

this community, although it is dispersed throughout Canada, has nonetheless kept its historic home, its main centre, its strongest and most dynamic support: Quebec. There, French-Canadians form a political society with its own powers and institutions and, above all, a state whose machinery and direction they control. This fact, of primary importance, adds a third dimension, that of politics and state, to the individual and cultural dimensions previously included in problem of equality. Finally aware of the dangers that confront it, and of the needs and aspirations of its people, Quebec has begun to demand equality not only at the individual and cultural level but also at the political level. Accordingly, Quebec demands powers which would make it master in its own house, and especially master of the policy that must be worked out for the French way of life within its territory.

Even if, however, the federal government declares its readiness to work toward linguistic and cultural equality—and this is the crucial point of the whole present debate—until now it has refused to consider Quebec as a special case. For it, Quebec is only a province like any other, and must be treated like the others. . . .

In short, English Canada and the federal government are inclined to grant French Canadians equality as individuals and perhaps also as a national community, but not equality as a political society: the only equality they are prepared to grant Quebec in this domain is equality with other provinces. The resulting situation raises a second question that is no less important than the first: equality *by* whom?

Equality by Whom?

The choice here is fundamental, and the nature of the choice arises largely from the reply we give to the first question: *for whom?* If we demand equality for the whole French-Canadian nation in all of Canada, it is obvious that the state of Quebec by itself is unable to guarantee and ensure this equality: it needs the co-operation of the central state and of the other provincial states. If, on the contrary, the equality we demand is limited to Quebec, it is no less obvious that the basic and essential role in this question will belong to the State of Quebec, which will discover therein fresh reasons for laying claim to full powers in everything that touches on the defence and advancement of French language and culture.

If we adopt this slogan, then, of "Equality or Independence," we must, if we want to be properly understood, make clear for whom we are making the demand. Are we talking about the French-Canadian nation as a whole? In this case the co-operation of other governments seems quite indispensable. As bad luck would have it, however, in the hundred years of federal rule which have just been completed, this co-operation has been refused by the provincial states and given only in a limited way by the central state. This has resulted in a condition of such inferiority, poverty, and insecurity for French life outside Quebec that many *Franco-Québécois* are now inclined to believe that there is no future for their language and culture except in Quebec and that, in consequence, all their efforts should go toward strengthening the Quebec State.

Is it still possible at least to show, if not to reverse, this train of thought which has more and more adherents in Quebec? For that, it would be necessary for the federal and other provincial governments to begin by giving some proof that they are sincerely interested in French life and inclined to accord it the same rights, the same chance, and the same treatment they have always accorded English language and culture. Even then, however, even if this condition were fulfilled, the problem would not be solved. In fact, it really seems that French life cannot be maintained outside Quebec without addition co-operation from the federal government, which would mean that the latter not only would have to retain the powers it already has in the linguistic and cultural fields, but would need new powers. Would the government of Quebec accept an increase in federal powers in areas it considers as belonging essentially to it? Would it, for the purpose of saving the French minorities, consent to a loss of its own powers? Or, to phrase it more generaly, in the hope that one day the French-Canadian community would enjoy political equality? Whether we conceive of this as taking the form of a Special Status, or that of an Associate State, or that of a completely Independent State, the problem remains essentially the same, for the solution in each of these cases implies from the very beginning a preference, a choice, an alternative in favour of Quebec.

Equality or independence: the alternative seems at first sight to represent a hard bargaining position. But as soon as we make an effort to go from theory to practice, the idea of equality raises almost as many questions as that of independence. What is more, when it is projected to take in specific requirements in the field of culture as well as politics, the idea of equality puts Quebec in motion directly along the path to sovereignty if not independence, so that in the end the two ideas of independence and equality are no longer in opposition but in full agreement. Equality for whom? And by whom? Until these two questions have received a clear answer, the debate will continue in ambiguity misinterpretation, and confusion. (Taken from an "Attempt at Clarification," by Richard Arès, s.j., *Relations*, November, 1967)

III FOR QUEBEC, IT IS ALL TOO CLEAR

At a time when some are trying to lead it astray into confusion, French Quebec itself is, literally, in danger of death. Several factors have been combining more quickly and more effectively than ever these last few years to emphasize the deterioration in our relative population strength.

First of all, the birth rate has decreased at a dizzying rate. It was 35.5 per 1,000 in 1921, and still 30.4 per 1,000 toward the end of the Second World War; but in 1961 it was down to 26.1, and it was barely over 21 in 1965. It is now under seventeen.

Thus the number of Quebec births fell to 120,609 in 1965, and to 113,423 in 1966. If we can believe the figures for the first eight months of the year, it has dropped again in 1967. (Quebec Bureau of Statistics, 1967)

Emigration, for its part, acts against us. In 1961, there were already 268,445 *Québécois* by birth living in other provinces, and we already have seen the rate of assimilation to which they are subject!

There are no accurate statistics covering emigration abroad; but we know that here, too, the loss is continuous and no less serious. Some studies estimate at one million the number of Canadians who left the country during the last twenty-five years, and it is more than likely that *Québécois* made up their "normal" share of this emigration.

Finally, there is immigration!

From 1945 to 1967 inclusive, Canada accepted some three million immigrants. More than thirty-five per cent, on the average, were of Anglo-Saxon origin.

As for the French, there were 4,408 of them out of 146,758

immigrants in 1965, or three per cent. In 1966, out of 194,743, there were 6,675 as opposed to 71,505 of British origin. And in 1967, while we reached in nine months a record of 170,000 immigrants thirty-five per cent of them Anglo-Saxon) we would have been lucky to have 10,000 French immigrants in the whole year. . . .

Nothing could be less surprising, for of thirty-five immigration offices six are in the United Kingdom and Ireland, five in Germany, and four in the United States. In living memory, there had been only a single office in France until Ottawa opened two new ones in 1966.

Moreover, countries and parts of the world which could provide excellent French-speaking applicants are completely neglected: no office in Latin America, in North Africa, in the Near East (except in Israel and Egypt), none whatever in the French-speaking areas of Asia.

The number employed in the various offices is also revealing. Thus, the Spanish office a short time ago had five employees, while the six British offices had an average of seventeen each, the five German offices twelve each.

We know the results of this policy in the rest of Canada. It had become a unilingual country where, in eight provinces at least, the French minorities are irreparably submerged.

As for Quebec, this policy combined with the falling birth rate is leading straight to a demographic catastrophe.

In mid-December of 1967, the Department of Immigration of Quebec revealed that of the 620,435 immigrants received between 1945 and 1966, about eighty per cent contributed to increasing the English-speaking population. In Montreal, "second largest French-speaking city in the world," the proportion was ninety per cent!

The newcomers of British origin alone (about 95,000) were twice those from France (about 50,000). And if we count the Germans (54,486), the Dutch (10,472), and the majority of the Americans (35,636), all of whom integrate "naturally" with the English-speaking group, we see the disproportionate number of those who, arriving in Quebec, already are, in practice, a part of the English language and culture group.

As for the remainder, the obvious English hegemony in our economic life, and our own inertia, quickly show them the direction to follow. . . .

We need only glance at the school situation in Montreal: in

1965, children of immigrants to Quebec made up thirty-five per cent of those attending Anglo-Protestant schools, sixty-four per cent (mainly Italians) of those attending Anglo-Catholic schools, and barely 3.5 per cent of the 170,000 children in the French schools! (Figures from the Montreal Catholic School Commission.)

As a large number of our regions have been undergoing severe *depopulation* for years now, while Montreal continues to be the most powerful magnet we possess, we can see easily where this threatens to lead us. The metropolis, even while continuously draining the population of other sectors of Quebec, has only a doubtful chance of maintaining the sixty-five per cent French-speaking population it counted in 1961.

Unless I am badly mistaken, this is a situation that is unique in the Western World. It emphasizes the quite abnormal structure of Quebec society, and the similarities of that society to others of a colonial type.

There is no place in the world where immigrants move spontaneously to join the minority, unless that minority is a dominant one.

But this is enough to see clearly where we stand and also what we must do, and do quickly.

In a very few years, it will be too late.*

Appendix **5** Association of Sovereign States

Let us now look a little more closely at the two examples that could provide the best inspiration for Quebec and the rest of Canada: those of the Scandinavian Union and the European Economic Community (the Common Market).

Keeping comment to a strict minimum of commentary, we will attempt to select only the most important facts, for they speak for themselves. It seems to us that by adapting for different circumstances as needed, we should find here a good many answers to the questions raised by our proposal.

*Unless otherwise indicated, information contained in the last section of this Appendix is taken from the *Basic Statements and Work Documents* of the Estates-General, published by Éditions de l'Action Nationale, 1967.

I THE SCANDINAVIAN UNION

The centre of this association—which is becoming a closer one as time goes by—is formed by the great peninsula on which Sweden and Norway lie side-by-side. These two countries have gone through precisely what Daniel Johnson has described as inconceivable in our case: *divorce after a century together, then a remarriage that is a growing success.* . . .

They had been united under the Swedish crown after 1815. Matters of war and peace, the making and breaking of treaties, the sending and receiving of diplomats were common to the two states.

But the Norwegians, fewer and poorer, felt they were considered second-class citizens. Toward the end of the nineteenth century, there were some ten years of more and more serious skirmishings. The moment of truth came over a conflict concerning diplomatic and consular agents: Norway wanted them to be organized independently by each of the united states. On May 23, 1905, the *Storthing* (parliament) of Norway voted a law setting up Norwegian consulates, but the King refused to sanction it. On June 7, after proclaiming the deposition of the sovereign, the Norwegian parliament declared the union dissolved. On August 13, the people approved the separation in a plebiscite (368,200 for, 184 against).

Sweden protested, but agreed to negotiate. At the end of August, 1905, Norwegian and Swedish delegates assembled in Karlstad to work out an amicable settlement.

This conference resulted in a whole series of agreements which, signed in Stockholm at the end of October that same year, set the scene for a healthy co-operation between formerly unhappy spouces who now had become free partners: an Agreement for settling differences by arbitration; an agreement on trade in transit; another on lakes and waterways common to both, etc. . . .

This partnership by mutual consent could only grow closer as time went on. The war of 1914-18 provided an occasion for enlarging the scope of the union when the King of Denmark joined those of Sweden and Norway in proclaiming the neutrality of the three countries. Finland and Iceland subsequently discovered their own family relationship with the initial trio, a relationship that was to grow continuously closer and more fruitful. Thus was formed a community of five nations, which were to build a joint pavilion at Expo 67 to illustrate their close bonds.

An Association of Unequals

In 1965, this block of five states had a total population of twenty million spread over two peninsulas and a northern island, with languages and cultures that were highly dissimilar and, at first sight, contained rather frightening differences.

Here, for example, are some vital statistics for that year for the four large countries in the community:

POPULATION thousands	G.N.P. Total, millions $ U.S.	G.N.P. per capita $ U.S.	WAGES hourly for men $ U.S.	BUDGET Spending in '66 Millions $ U.S.	POLITICAL SYSTEM
SWEDEN 7,734	19,306	2,496	2.03	5,622	MONARCHY Soc.-Dem.
NORWAY 3,723	7,002	1,881	1.61	1,671	MONARCHY Centre-Cons.
DENMARK 4,748	9,985	2,099	1.63	2,266	MONARCHY Soc.-Dem.
FINLAND 4,612	8,119	1,760	1.44	2,013	REPUBLIC Coalition/ Left

Increasing Co-operation

Here, now, is a glance at the increasingly closer bonds that unite these quite different states, as described by the Nordic Council, a consultative body set up in 1952 for the *five* countries:

The Nordic Council is composed of sixty-nine elected members, with sixteen each from the Danish, Finnish, Norwegian, and Swedish parliaments and five from the parliament of Iceland. In addition, representatives of the governments—normally about thirty-five—are present without right of vote in Council sessions, which thus have an attendance of about one hundred. The Council meets annually for a week's session.

The Bureau, the Secretariat, and the five Commissions into which the elected members are divided meet several times between sessions and proceed to the examination of proposals which came from Council members and at times from the governments themselves. The governments in their actions take into account most of the recommendations formulated by the

Council. Inter-governmental contracts are ensured by ministerial conferences which are held at regular intervals in the various areas of business. For the most important sectors such as economics, agriculture, legislation, or the labour market, the governments have set up permanent committees which for the most part report on their work to the Nordic Council. The various administrative bodies hold Nordic conferences at regular intervals. Finally, the national administrative bodies operating in the same fields maintain contact with one another either by telephone or by correspondence. In the different ministries a "liaison man" is specifically charged with Nordic matters. . . .

Transportation and Communication

In the field of transportation, inter-Nordic co-operation has enabled major results to be achieved, thanks to the creation of the Scandinavian Airlines System (SAS), which is a merger of three airlines, the Danish, Norwegian, and Swedish. The SAS has become an international company whose lines serve the four corners of the world; it is of great help to the Nordic group in holding its place in international aviation.

The Nordic countries form a union so far as passports are concerned, in the sense that passport control does not exist at inter-Nordic frontiers, either for subjects of the two countries or those of other member States.

Labour and Social Security

The Nordic countries constitute a unified manpower market, within which the worker, in the broadest sense of the term, need not obtain residential or work permits. These countries are making every effort to extend this freedom to certain professions whose practice is subject to a particular authority or control. They have signed agreements for a Nordic work market for doctors and dentists. Other agreements are being studied for pharmacists, nurses, and psychotherapists. The major agreement on social security signed in 1955 gives to all Nordic subjects the right to the same social benefits as those enjoyed by nationals of the Nordic country in which they are residents or immigrants.

Legislation

For almost a century now, the Nordic countries have been attempting to bring their national laws into harmony. Of special importance is the work undertaken in this regard in commercial law, particularly in the fields of sales and patents. Persons convicted of crimes can serve their time in their own country, and the rules of procedure for inter-Nordic extradition have been simplified. On many points these countries are united more closely than the states of certain confederations.

Each of the states allows naturalization of other Nordic nationals more quickly than for subjects of non-member states (five years waiting period instead of seven). Projects are underway to facilitate further the inter-acquisition of Nordic nationalities. . . .

Culture, Education, and Research

Co-operation in research and higher education takes on special importance because of the fact that scientific progress has a direct influence on technical improvements and economic development, and, as a consequence, on the standard of living. Co-operation for rational use of common resources has been instituted in different specialized fields, either by creating an institution common to the Nordic group or by co-ordinating projects and dividing them among the different countries of the group. The most important of these institutions are the following: Nordic Institute of Theoretical Physics (Copenhagen), the Nordic School of Journalism (Aarhus), the Nordic School of Higher Studies in Hygiene (Göteborg), the Nordic Institute of Maritime Law (Oslo), the Nordic Institute of Folklore (Copenhagen), the Nordic Institute of African Studies (Upsala), and the Nordic Institute of Asian Studies (Copenhagen). Other institutes co-operate in the fields of biological oceanography, household science, and criminology.

As a supplement to the activities of the inter-Nordic institutions and the co-ordination of scientific research, scholarships promote the exchanges of professors, young scientists, and students. A system of equivalent of diplomas has been created for a certain faculties, and every effort is being made to extend this program.

Radio and Television

The Nordic broadcasting agencies have frequent program exchanges. One agency in particular, Nordvision, was set up to facilitate production and exchange of television programmes. . . .

In short, Scandinavian solidarity has become so strong that in a number of areas these sovereign states are closer to each other than are the members of a good many federal unions!

And all this has been accomplished freely, without the influence of any supra-national authority.

(This is equally true of Benelux, where it should be emphasized that supra-national institutions *would be all the more unnecessary as there are only two contracting parties to the Association*: Holland and the Belgio-Luxemburg Union.)

II THE EUROPEAN ECONOMIC COMMUNITY

Much has been said since 1945 about the "German miracle," and somewhat more recently about the Italian miracle; less has been said of the French miracle, although its existence is just as real.

But the real miracle, encompassing all these prodigies, is that of Europe itself. Even if we take into account the massive aid received from the United States under the Marshall Plan program after the war, there is still nothing more miraculous than the resurgence of this old Europe out of the abyss of ruins, demoralization, and hate into which it had hurled itself for the previous five years. What greater miracle than to see nations, separated twenty-five years ago by veritable seas of blood, reunited within this Economic Community because of which, in fact, they have both individually and collectively achieved swifter and surer progress than ever in the past!

At the outset, however, this "common market" inspired terror in many of those who have since benefited the most from it: for example, the French industrialists, who were afraid of being "swallowed" by their powerful German counterparts; and little Benelux, with its twenty million people, not sure that it could keep pace with associates at least twice as large. . . .

Ten years later everyone long since had forgotten these initial terrors. The unknown factor of yesterday now is the increasingly stable framework in which new institutions (which quickly grew familiar) have provided unprecedented progress to six ancient and still sovereign peoples who dared to make to take the plunge into well-ordered interdependence.

The backbone of this miracle is the Treaty of Rome, signed on March 25, 1957.

We reproduce now some of its most important clauses—
clauses that are by analogy the most instructive for us. . . .*

Principles

Article 2
It shall be the aim of the Community, by establishing a Common
Market and progressively approximating the economic policies
of Member States, to promote throughout the Community a
harmonious development of economic activities, a continuous
and balanced expansion, an increased stability, an accelerated
raising of the standard of living and closer relations between its
Member States.

Article 3
For the purposes set out in the preceding Article, the activities
of the Community shall include, under the conditions and with
the timing provided for in this Treaty:
a / the elimination, as between Member States, of customs duties
and of quantitative restrictions in regard to the importation and
exportation of goods, as well as of all other measures with
equivalent effect;
b / the establishment of a common customs tariff and a common
commercial policy towards third countries;
c / the abolition, as between Member States, of the obstacles to
the free movement of persons, services, and capital;
d / the inauguration of a common agricultural policy;
e / the inauguration of a common transport policy;
f / the establishment of a system ensuring that competition shall
not be distorted in the Common Market;
g / the application of procedures which shall make it possible to
co-ordinate the economic policies of Member States and to
remedy disequilibria in their balances of payments;
h / the approximation of their respective municipal law to the
extent necessary for the functioning of the Common Market;
i / the creation of a European Social Fund in order to improve
the possibilities of employment for workers and to contribute
to the raising of their standard of living;

*The complete text of the 248 articles, followed by a number of
protocols and conventions, can be found in *Treaty establishing the
European Economic Community*, published by the Secretariat of the
Interim Committee of the Common Market and Euratom, Brussels.

j / the establishment of a European Investment Bank intended to facilitate the economic expansion of the Community through the creation of new resources; and

k / the association of overseas countries and territories with the Community with a view to increasing trade and to pursuing jointly their effort towards economic and social development.

Article 4

1 / The achievement of the tasks entrusted to the Community shall be ensured by:

- —an ASSEMBLY;
- —a COUNCIL;
- —a COMMISSION;
- —a COURT OF JUSTICE.

Each of these institutions shall act within the limits of the powers conferred upon it by this Treaty.

2 / The Council and the Commission shall be assisted by an Economic and Social Committee acting in a consultative capacity.

Article 5

Member States shall take all general or particular measures which are appropriate for ensuring the carrying out of the obligations arising out of this Treaty or resulting from the acts of the institutions of the Community. They shall facilitate the achievement of the Community's aims.

They shall abstain from any measures likely to jeopardize the attainment of the objectives of this Treaty.

Article 6

1 / Member States, acting in close collaboration with the institutions of the Community, shall co-ordinate their respective economic policies to the extent that is necessary to attain the objectives of this Treaty.

2 / The institutions of the Community shall take care not to prejudice the internal and external financial stability of Member States.

The Basic Institutions of the Community

Article 9

1 / The Community shall be based upon a customs union covering the exchange of all goods and comprising both the prohibition, as between Member States, of customs duties on importation and exportation and all charges with equivalent effect and the adoption of a common customs tariff in their relations with third countries. . . .

Article 137
The Assembly, which shall be composed of representatives of the States united within the Community, shall exercise the powers of deliberation and of control which are conferred upon it by this Treaty.

Article 138
1/The Assembly shall be composed of delegates whom the Parliaments shall be called upon to appoint from among their members in accordance with the procedure laid down by each Member State. . . .

Article 145
With a view to ensuring the achievement of the objectives laid down in this Treaty, and under the conditions provided for therein, the Council shall:

—ensure the co-ordination of the general economic policies of the Member States; and

—dispose of a power of decision.

Article 146
The Council shall be composed of representatives of the Member States. Each Government shall delegate to it one of its members.

The office of President shall be exercised for a term of six months by each member of the Council in rotation according to the alphabetical order of the Member States.

Article 155
With a view to ensuring the functioning and development of the Common Market, the Commission shall:

—ensure the application of the provisions of this Treaty and of the provisions enacted by the institutions of the Community in pursuance thereof;

—formulate recommendations or opinions in matters which are the subject of this Treaty, where the latter expressly so provides or where the Commission consider it necessary;

—under the conditions laid down in this Treaty dispose of a

power of decision of its own and participate in the preparation of acts of the Council and of the Assembly; and
—exercise the competence conferred on it by the Council for the implementation of the rules laid down by the latter.

Article 157

1 / The Commission shall be composed of nine members chosen for their general competence and of indisputable independence.

The number of members of the Commission may be amended by a unanimous vote of the Council.

Only nationals of Member States may be members of the Commission.

The Commission may not include more than two members having the nationality of the same State.

2 / The members of the Commission shall perform their duties in the general interest of the Community with complete independence.

In that performance of their duties, they shall not seek or accept instructions from any Government or other body. They shall refrain from any action incompatible with the character of their duties. Each Member State undertakes to respect this character and not to seek to influence the members of the Commission in the performance of their duties. . . .

Article 164

The Court of Justice shall ensure observance of law and justice in the interpretation and application of this Treaty.

Article 165

The Court of Justice shall be composed of seven judges. . . .

Article 171

If the Court of Justice finds that a Member State has failed to fulfil any of its obligations under this Treaty, such State shall take the measures required for the implementation of the judgment of the Court.

Agriculture

Article 39

1 / The common agricultural policy shall have as its objectives:
a / to increase agricultural productivity by developing technical

progress and by ensuring the rational development of agricultural production and the optimum utilization of the factors of production, particularly labour;

b/ to ensure thereby a fair standard of living for the agricultural population, particularly by the increasing of the individual earnings of persons engaged in agriculture;

c/ to stabilize markets;

d/ to guarantee regular supplies; and

e/ to ensure reasonable prices in supplies to consumers.

2/ In working out the common agricultural policy and the special methods which it may involve, due account shall be taken of:

a/ the particular character of agricultural activities, arising from the social structure of agriculture and from structural and natural disparities between the various agricultural regions;

b/ the need to make the appropriae adjustments gradually; and

c/ the fact that in Member States agriculture constitutes a sector which is closely linked with the economy as a whole.

Article 40

1/ Member States shall gradually develop the common agricultural policy during the transitional period and shall establish it not later than at the end of that period.

2/ With a view to achieving the objectives set out in Article 39, a common organization of agricultural markets shall be effected.

This organisation shall take one of the following forms according to the products concerned:

a/ common rules concerning competition;

b/ compulsory co-ordination of the various national market organisations; or

c/ a European market organization.

3/ The common organization in one of the forms mentioned in Paragraph 2 may comprise all measures necessary to achieve the objectives set out in Article 39, in particular, price controls, subsides as to the production and marketing of various products, arrangements for stock-piling and carry-forward, and common machinery for stabilizing importation or exportation.

The organisation shall confine itself to pursuing the objectives set out in Article 39 and shall exclude any discrimination between producers or consumers within the Community.

A common price policy, if any, shall be based on common criteria and on uniform methods of calculation.

4 / In order to enable the common organization referred to in Paragraph 2 to achieve its objectives, one or more agricultural orientation and guarantee funds may be established.

Workers

Article **48**

1 / The free movement of workers shall be ensured within the Community not later than at the date of the expiry of the transitional period.

2 / This shall involve the abolition of any discrimination based on nationality between workers of the Member States as regards employment, remuneration, and other working conditions.

3 / It shall include the right, subject to limitations justified by reasons of public order, public safety, and public health:

a / to accept offers of employment actually made;

b / to move about freely for this purpose within the territory of Member States;

c / to stay in any Member State in order to carry on an employment in conformity with the legislative and administrative provisions governing the employment of the workers of that State; and

d / to live, on conditions which shall be the subject of implementing regulations to be laid down by the Commission, in the territory of a Member State after having been employed there.

4 / The provisions of this Article shall not apply to employment in nthe public administration.

Article **52**

Within the framework of the provisions set out below, restrictions on the freedom of establishment of nationals of a Member State in the territory of another Member State shall be progressively abolished in the course of the transitional period. Such progressive abolition shall also extend to restrictions on the setting up of agencies, branches, or subsidiaries by nationals of any Member State established in the territory of any Member State.

Freedom of establishment shall include the right to engage in and carry on non-wage-earning activities, and also to set up and manage enterprises and, in particular, companies within the meaning of Article 58, Paragraph 2, under the conditions laid down by the provisions of the Chapter relating to capital.

Capital

Article 67

1 / Member States shall, in the course of the transitional period and to the extent necessary for the proper functioning of the Common Market, progressively abolish as between themselves restrictions on the movement of capital belonging to persons resident in Member States and also any discriminatory treatment based on the nationality or place of residence of the parties or on the place in which such capital is invested.

2 / Current payments connected with movements of capital between Member States shall be freed from all restrictions not later than at the end of the first stage.

Transport

Article 74

The objectives of this Treaty shall, with regard to the subject covered by this Title, be pursued by the Member States within the framework of a common transport policy.

Article 75

1 / With a view to implementing Article 74 and taking due account of the special aspects of transport, the Council, acting on a proposal of the Commission and after the Economic and Social Committee and the Assembly have been consulted, shall, until the end of the second stage by means of a unanimous vote and subsequently by means of a qualified majority vote, lay down:

a / common rules applicable to international transport effected from or to the territory of a Member State or crossing the territory of one or more Member States;

b / conditions for the admission of non-resident carriers to national transport services within a Member State; and

c / any other appropriate provisions.

2 / The provisions referred to under (a) and (b) of the preceding paragraph shall be laid down in the course of the transitional period. . . .

Harmonization of Laws

Article 100

The Council, acting by means of a unanimous vote on a proposal of the Commission, shall issue directives for the "rapprochement" of such legislative and administrative provisions of the Member States as have a direct incidence on the establsh-ment or functioning of the Common Market.

The Assembly and the Economic and Social Committee shall be consulted concerning any directives whose implemen-tation in one or more of the Member States would involve amendment of legislative provision.

Instead of Equalization Payments

Article 129

A European Investment Bank having legal personality shall hereby be established.

The members of the European Investment Bank shall be the Member States.

The Statute of the European Investment Bank shall form the subject of a Protocol annexed to this Treaty.

Article 130

The task of the European Investment Bank shall be to con-tribute, by calling on the capital markets and its own resources, to the balanced and smooth development of the Common Market in the interest of the Community. For this purpose, the Bank shall by granting loans and guarantees on a non-profit-making basis facilitate the financing of the following projects in all sectors of the economy:

a / projects for developing less-developed regions,

b / projects for modernizing or converting enterprises or for creating new activities which are called for by the progressive establishment of the Common Market where such projects by their size or nature cannot be entirely financed by the various means available in each of the Member States; and

c / projects of common interest to several Member States which by their size or nature cannot be entirely financed by the various means available in each of the Member States.

General Provisions

Article 212

The Council, acting by means of a unanimous vote, shall, in collaboration with the Commission and after consulting the other institutions concerned, lay down the statute of service for officials and the conditions of employment for other employees of the Community. . . .

Article **216**
The seat of the Community's institutions shall be fixed by the Governments of the Member States acting in common agreement.

Article **235**
If any action by the Community appears necessary to achieve, in the functioning of the Common Market, one of the aims of the community in cases where this Treaty has not provided for the requisite powers of action, the Council, acting by means of a unanimous vote on a proposal of the Commission and after the Assembly has been consulted, shall enact the appropriate provisions.

Article **236**
The Government of any Member State or the Commission may submit to the Council proposals for the revision of this Treaty.

   If the Council, after consulting the Assembly and, where appropriate, the Commission, expresses an opinion in favour of the calling of a conference of representatives of the Governments of Member States, such conference shall be convened by the President of the Council for the purpose of determining in common agreement the amendments to be made to this Treaty.

   Such amendments shall enter into force after being ratified by all Member States in accordance with their respective constitutional rules.

Article **240**
This Treaty shall be concluded for an unlimited period.

Appendix **6** Other Testimony

Sovereignty, Condition of Salvation
by Jean-Marc Léger

Contemporary society no longer permits the existence of isolated sectors of legislation; moreover, the natural evolution of things —natural and often desirable—is bringing about a continual extension of the scope of State intervention. This modern state is an infinitely complex mechanism where everything is related to everything else, where social security, for example, is at least as involved with economic policy as it is with welfare policy; where manpower policy involves control of training and, progressively, of all education; where radio and television broadcasting are as much a means of education as schools, if not more; where, by the interplay of international organizations and agreements, foreign policy which now touches on all the larger realms of human activity) has increasing direct and daily repercussions on internal policy. A state that desires to develop normally must be able to act simultaneously in all these domains, or sooner or later it will be completely paralyzed. A state that wants to act efficiently today must be able to intervene and legislate in all of these areas.

The Permanent Collision Between Ottawa and Quebec

If this is granted, how can there be anything but a permanent collision between the normal aspirations of Quebec and the no less normal aspirations of the central government? At a given point one or the other must give in. A "strong Quebec in a strong Canada" may be a clever slogan, but it can be only the cloak for a sucker's game. . . .

Let us leave aside for the moment the expressions "independence" and "special status." Let us simply ask the question: what is essential to a nation desirous of developing naturally in the modern world, and of doing so according to its own aspirations and in the light of its own culture? It must be able to act continuously upon four or five essential elements of its life: demographic growth, cultural growth, the best possible use of its human resources (and the protection of those resources), the putting in order of its territory and its habitat, the means to adapt constantly to change and, obviously, the financial resources needed for the implementation of such policies. These are the things, moreover, that run like a filigree through the programs of even of non-separatist groups such as the Liberal Party of Quebec and the Union Nationale.

Demographic growth, for example, presupposes authority in immigration matters; cultural growth calls for control of broadcasting and schools, among other things; the best use of human resources involves control of manpower policy and adult education; the protection of human resources presupposes total control of social security, etc. The most moderate of "quiet revolutions" can not logically ignore these needs. But these demands are basically incompatible with Canadian federalism, with the latter's source of inspiration, and above all with the kind of development to which our times are pushing it. Messrs. Trudeau and Lamontagne have at least had the honesty to proclaim the fact. Those who tell us that "Quebec can satisfy all its aspirations within confederation" (revamped or otherwise) are deceiving themselves or, in some cases, deceiving us. They are either reducing Quebec's aspirations to insignificance (a slightly higher percentage of direct taxes, the right to sign cultural agreements abroad, a little more bilingualism in Ottawa); or they have no understanding of the modern State and the evolution of the Canadian federal system.

We are moving toward a federation which in its essentials is bound to grow more and more centralized, even under the cautious and nicely wrapped formulas of "co-operative federalism" or the theory of not-totally-distinctive "grey areas"; even if it brings concessions to Quebec particularism in minor matters along with a good dose of bilingualism to allow Ottawa's neo-interventionism to get by.

Nothing is more revealing in this respect than the speech by Maurice Lamontagne quoted above, a speech as frank as it is intelligent. The progress and unity of Canada more and more will require a strong central state, and Ottawa can not stand outside of any of the great areas of policy which determine the future of the country and the quality of its citizens: education, science, manpower and the exploitation of natural resources, improvement of the land, cultural affairs, or a rebirth of new life into its negelected regions, along with the expansion of social security. Co-operation, consultation, decentralization in the application of policies—as much as you like of these, but there will be one boss: Ottawa.

Special Status is Inacceptable

There will never be a special status in the sense understood by those *Québécois* who belive that this is where the solution lies: the sort of basic minimum described by *Le Devoir* in its supplement of June 30, 1967, is inacceptable to Ottawa. Lamontagne said as much, and by his own standards he is perfectly right: Canadian federalism cannot accommodate itself to such a special status. We might see the title or the shadow of it, but never the thing itself. To try at the same time for special status and for true federation is like trying to square the circle.

Power relationships at every level make the notion of equality between the French- and English-speaking nations in Canada as illusory as the old dream of equality of language and culture. Canadian federalism, by virtue of its origin, its inspiration, and especially its present direction, cannot conceivably tolerate a true special status for Quebec; it has very reason, on the contrary, to pursue an increase in centralization and uniformity.

Federation is a dead-end street for Quebec; given time, it will inevitably be the graveyard of the French-Canadian nation. . . .

True Life or Slow Death

For Quebec today the choice is not between two systems more or less favourable to its overall progress. The choice is simply one between a good life and a slow death. And we cannot play hide-and-seek with history by saying, "We aren't ready yet. . . . but we will be in fifteen, twenty or twenty-five years." There is very little chance that in a quarter of a century we will still be free to choose. The factors that supposedly conspire today against independence will be ten or twenty times more powerful then, and today's impetus toward independence will be measurably weakned. For Canada is devouring Quebec: demographically, economically, constitutionally, culturally. There will come a time when the gravity of the problems and the deterioration of the situation will be such that radical action must be taken; but when we finally do realize this we no longer will have the moral or physical strength for the necessary effort.

The Last Chance

The truth is that we are a people in danger of death, and we now have, doubtless for the last time in our history, the opportunity for a genuine choice on the most essential point. It is childish to think that we can plan our collective future in the way one plans the various stages of building some industrial complex: that we might first try out the "special-status" solution for ten years or so, after which we could go on to the system of associate states for another decade and finally, if circumstances seemed favourable, proclaim our independence. It certainly would take less than ten years before French Canada would have to choose between life and death, between having a fatherland and consenting to a slow submersion in the Anglo-Saxon sea.

A Life of Dignity and Co-operation for Quebec and Canada

Far from being the daydream or the mad adventure that some would call it, independence is at the same time the only logical result of our situation and the absolute pre-condition for a natural life. Without its inspiration the struggle for survival would be only a rear-guard action, an odious deception. If we can control our irrational reflexes of conservatism and false sentiment, we will recognize that the independence of Quebec and Canada represent (in a world of diversity and interdependence) a formula of dignity and reason and our great chance for organic co-operation. Tomorrow English Canada would be grateful to Quebec for bringing it about.

For Quebec, in fact, independence is a vital necessity; for Canada, Quebec's independence is the prerequisite to a fuller development. For the two states this would provide a new and fruitful start. For we are a dead weight on English Canada, and we ourselves lead a mutilated existence. Canada in its present form is condemned to mediocrity. In a permanent atmosphere of mistrust, bad-humour, and general dissatisfaction, what do we find? An endless series of delicate and crippled compromises, negotiations forever underway on age-old problems and new situations, a shocking waste of time, money, and talent in attempts to hold the pieces together and, above all, to preserve the illusion in the weaker of the two partners that he is "just as equal as the other." Does anyone believe that a country can survive and progress in the atmosphere that has prevailed for the last few years? And things are not about to improve, for the requirements of our time and the natural inclinations of the Anglo-Saxons will lead to increased centralization. And at every stage this will be less favourable for Quebec, until the day when its very name no longer expresses a distinct entity, for the Franco-Quebec nation will have become a minority in its own home.

Fifteen years of difficult discussions between ministers of justice and heads of governments were needed to reach a difficult agreement on the simple matter of amending the constitution—an agreement which Quebec was finally to discard. At the most optimistic estimate, Quebec would need twenty-five years of negotiations to obtain an *ersatz* special status (and by that time, in the year 2000, the probable English-speaking majority in Quebec, made up of Britons and anglicized New-Quebeckers, would not even want such a special status). Quebec and English Canada will expand great amounts of energy in this melancholy and disappointing struggle, while the great tasks of development and social and cultural progress stand crying for action, in a merciless world where, once we have fallen behind, it is more and more difficult to catch up. This federation has the cross of death on its forehead, and we share this doubtful decoration. To be sure, it can survive a few more decades if the two nations are willing to go on with their sterile game of squaring the circle, and if the French-Canadian nation agrees to its own slow disappearance and gives up any idea of acquiring the tools to create its own future.

If the people of Quebec, adopting the terms of the preamble to the American Declaration of Independence, should be asked to "declare the causes which persuade it to independence," it would be obliged to add to the "free right of peoples to self-determination" another reason: the slow suicide that membership in this federation means to us. Under siege for so long, our nation now is under attack: its economic position is continually worsening, not only in Canada as a whole but in Quebec itself. The masses of immigrants arriving in its territory add the weight of their numbers to the English-speaking minority (who would, without them, amount to eight or nine per cent rather than twenty or twenty-one per cent). The use of the French language, and its usefulness, recede continually, especially in Montreal. We are on the way to losing Montreal, if we have not already done so, and the rot in the metropolis, the cancer of French Canada, is an indication of what will happen tomorrow in all Quebec.

Only a sovereign state can exercise absolute control over immigration policy or make French into the necessary language –*i.e.,* the only language–officially and in practice. Only a sovereign state can institute the psychological climate and set up the structures indispensable to economic emancipation and development-planning in the interests of the *Québécois*. Only a sovereign state can integrate broadcasting with a national educational and cultural policy that is determined and progressive. And, finally, only a sovereign state can carry out a policy of foreign relations as a function of the cultural and material interests of Quebec society allowing the latter to participate as

an adult nation in the great movement of international co-operation. These tools for action – to name only these – are all equally
indispensable: if only one is lacking, the whole edifice is
endangered.

When a nation sees ninety per cent of its immigrants join
the ranks of the minority and adopt the latter's language and go
to its schools, when a nation must resign itself to the fact that
the majority of its sons work in a foreign language in their own
country, when a nation does not even control twenty per cent of
the economic activity in its own territory, it is not only gravely
ill, it is threatened with extinction. If it does not quickly change
the conditions that have given rise to such a state of affairs, it
will be able to do more than fill the breaches, which will continue to gape wider and wider, trying to stem the forward march
of an inexorable process. But the tools of our collective salvation are incompatible with any diminished status whatsoever,
with any "special" status whatsoever – (the latter being, moreover, illusory and at the same time incompatible with federalism): the tools of salvation can be found only in national independence.

The Canadian federation represents for Quebec a kind of
frightful myth of Sisyphus: the principal threats and evils denounced today already were denounced a century ago; then,
with more force, fifty years ago, and again twenty-five years ago.
They persist today in a form that is more critical than ever. And
the acceleration of history, more notable then in any other era,
can only make the process more speedy.

The *Franco-Québécois* society is becoming a minority before our very eyes. If the present regime persists, we will soon
be the "largest French-speaking minority" in Canada. As for
what would come next, we need only consult our "minorities"
in the other provinces, minorities which, according to some, we
of the independence movement want to abandon. But what has
Quebec been able to do, as a province of Canada, toward defending and promoting the welfare of these minorities over the
last century? If they have any future, it will be through the
sovereignty of Quebec, *i.e.,* through the existence of a French-
speaking state whose influence, means of action and, if necessary, pressure will be infinitely more useful to them than any
number of petitions, friendship visits and subscriptions.

Quebec can only look on helplessly at the process of assimilation which is alienating an increasing number of French-speaking communities in the rest of the country. We are expected to share their lot, no doubt as an act of sympathy. The independence of Quebec would be the only real help we could offer to these minority groups, through an agreement on the reciprocal treatment of minorities which Quebec could propose to Canada, bringing to bear the normal weight and effectiveness of a sovereign state (including its international resources). And perhaps the greatest encouragement we could offer our minorities would be the true homeland that would be available to all French-speaking groups in America.

But it is not only a question of satisfying a normal aspiration, nor of avoiding the destiny of being reduced to the level of a group quaintly interesting for its folklore values but destined to assimilation. It is also, and perhaps primarily, a question of founding in America a modern and progressive society that is distinct from the modern Minotaur, the U.S.A. This society's first concern would have to be the human progress of the masses of Quebec, which today are in complete disarray. By the healthy shock it will create, and the new psychological climate it will establish, independence will be the first step in an authentic "quiet revolution," for that revolution is not worth undertaking if it consists merely of sticking new labels on social and cultural facts and attitudes which remain unchanged. A sovereign Quebec first and foremost must represent an act of liberation and progress for the masses, who must be given back a consciousness of their dignity and culture. It is the promotion of these in every sphere that must be the primary objective of independence.

Independence: A Point of Departure

For independence is not a final achievement but merely a point of departure. Its actual embodiment will come about through the building of a new society, and through a concern for the human values which today, like democracy and liberty, tend to take refuge in small nations. In short, national sovereignty will be springtime for Quebec, after the exhausting and monotonous winter of a grey and mediocre era of bare survival.

In this world of innovation and change which has, in the last few decades, undergone immense and often unforeseen political and social unheavals, where an effort is being made to reconcile the need for human dignity with that of efficiency (*i.e.*, national liberty with international co-operation), why should Quebec's independence—and Quebec's alone—be something abnormal or shocking or dangerous, almost monstrous? It would be harmful perhaps to certain interests and to the traditional "establishment," but it would not be a true threat to anyone. It would be good for both Quebec and Canada. The former needs it simply to live, the latter in order to live better.

Of all the rights that are recognized—or at least proclaimed —by twentieth-century man, is there a more fundamental one than the right to a genuine homeland, the right to live (and hence to work) in one's own language, the right to have a daily environment in harmony with one's culture and mentality, the right to take part in the concert of nations freely and directly? This is known as freely choosing and creating one's destiny: it is known as independence. Dignity and reason urge us to take this path, all the more forcefully because by taking it we preserve for ourselves and for "the others" those things which are today the most essential: liberty, expansion, and co-operation. For Quebec and for Canada this is an historic opportunity to be seized together in the common interest. On the other hand, if Canada is to be progressively absorbed by its great neighbour, is it not important for that part of Canada with the greatest chance of resisting (and the greatest significance) to detach itself while there is still time, to preserve at least one independent voice in North America and to ensure that this voice is not just the echo *de jure* or *de facto,* of the u.s.a.?

Dignity and liberty are not things for which one begs: one deserves them and fights for them, or rather one deserves them through fighting for them. Quebec will never survive or develop if its survival and development are left to the goodwill, the benevolence or the sympathy of the Anglo-Saxon world, however real and widespread these might be. It will exist and grow only by its own actions and—most important—by its own choice. The coming time is one for courage, and also one for lucidity and fervour.

A state which is economically free, socially just, culturally progressive, and politically sovereign: this is what Quebec should be, and its citizens should be assured of the benefits of such a state. This can come about only through full independence, along with many varieties of organic co-operation with its neighbours. The objective can still be decided and attained.

If Quebec denies itself this, let's at least find some good arguments to justify such "living" on borrowed time.*

QUEBEC'S INDEPENDENCE

*Condition of Quebec's Salvation,
Guarantee of Peace for Canada*
by Doris Lussier

*The more I look at the present situation of our people in Quebec
and in Canada, the more I confirm my deep conviction that for
the French-Canadian nation independence is a matter of life
and death. In saying this I am not indulging in romantic
nationalism, I am expressing a truth in the field of political
science. Either Quebec chooses and organizes its political independence—in which case the nation has a chance of living as
such and flourishing in prosperous freedom; or Quebec stays in
Confederation—in which case the nation certainly will move
toward the gentle death of progressive assimilation and submersion in the English-speaking sea.*

English-Canadians Know This

*English-Canadians know it. We should not take them for fools,
after all. Their leaders see perfectly well that according to the
pattern of Canadian economic development they need only wait
another hundred years and, lo and behold, assimilation is an
accomplished fact. The Quebec nation will be irreversibly caught
in a fatal process of gradual extinction which soon would put
it into the museum of Canadian history.*

*And it is because they know this that they are so fond of
the* status quo *of Confederation. This is why they attempt, with
all the weight of their dominant majority, to postpone the
moment of constitutional change. They know very well—and
understand better than we do—that political independence for
Quebec is our only hope. And they will do everything they can
to temporize, prolong discussions, put off, play the game of
compromise, giving in a little and postponing a lot, aware as
they are that our death by quiet assimilation will come of its
own accord, like a gift of destiny and a smile from History. . . .*

*The facts I have just outlined are undisputed. Using them
as starting-points, and aware of their cultural nature, the French-*

*Selected from articles published in *Le Devoir*, October 2, 3, 24, and
25, 1967. Sub-titles are not all the author's.

Canadian nation must choose the path of its future. It is now or never. We are going through the exhilarating and awesome hour of our final chance.

The time when we were politically under-age is past. From now on and forever our nation wants to live as an adult. If we want to remain French, if we want to conduct our lives in French, like a normal nation, there is no path to take other than that which leads to the "political sovereignty of Quebec, along with an economic Union with the rest of Canada." This means independence without total separation. This means freedom from our perpetual minority status to associate ourselves in true liberty and equality [with English Canada].

Between Civilized Humans

For we must also say to those who see in our independence a reason for systematic hostility by English Canada that they know very little of the psychology of nations, and still less about either the English- or French-Canadian psyche. We are two traditionally peaceful nations who have lived together in relative but genuine peace for two hundred years. It will not be the fact that we want to associate with them on other terms than those of our present political contract that will turn the English-Canadians into Huns or make them want to destroy us. No. They are civilized and, above all, practical people. I am sure that with the passing of the first understandable emotions aroused by our accession to independence, they will see that beyond the differences that separate us culturally—the differences that lead us to choose distinct political systems—there remains and always will remain a community of interests—spiritual as well as material—which make it worthwhile to work together in a new context in order to safeguard and develop those interests.

I firmly believe, moreover, that English Canadians and Québécois will be better friends if they live side-by-side like good neighbours, each in his own house, than they are now in the confines of a home whose construction leads to constant bickering and a life of perpetual mutual frustration.

The independence of Quebec is not only the condition of salvation for the French-Canadian nation; it is the best guarantee of peace for Canada.*

*Excerpts from an interview in *Echos-Vedettes*, November 11, 1967.

Appendix **7** **Operation Panic**

(Or: How to "Help Along" the Flight of Capital . . .)

Beyond doubt, there was some flight of capital from Quebec in October and November, 1967.

It was neither the first nor the last time such a thing had happened. According to circumstances, similar and more-or-less serious flights of capital are bound to occur under any political regime. (In almost all countries the most decisive contributory circumstances are usually beyond their control.)

It is nevertheless important—*and very edifying*—to trace the cause and extent of these capital movements in the autumn of 1967.

Let us recall the course of events. On September 18, the manifesto of our future movement was made public by René Lévesque. This was interpreted as a political gesture forming part of a nationalist escalation in which the [provincial] government has not been entirely inactive. This manifesto subsequently was held responsible for having caused a deterioration in the financial "climate" of Quebec.

At just about the same time, however, it became apparent that the Congress of the United States was about to reject the tax increase requested by President Johnson. Faced with the prospect of massive loans to the American government to finance the war in Vietnam, the New York bond market collapsed and dragged down with it every North American market, including those in Montreal and Toronto. The price of Quebec bonds dropped, as others did, and their yield increased. The government of Quebec was obliged to borrow at increasingly high rates.

To ascertain whether the effect on Quebec bonds was more or less serious than that on other government bonds, we can chart each day the daily gap in yield rates between the various issues. For some time it had been noted the yield rate of Quebec bonds was normally about one per cent higher than that of Canadian government bonds, and about 0.5% higher than that of Ontario bonds. At mid-September, the differences were about of this order.

Until October 13, things remained the same. The differences remained constant. The market was very slow. The North American slump was general and applied in more-or-less equal degree everywhere.

The manifesto of September 18 has, however, produced other reactions. The owners of certain bank accounts, made nervous by the escalation of declarations, transferred their accounts from Montreal to Toronto. This was of very little consequence and in any case did not affect the price of Quebec bonds which, one might think, would have been the first to react.

An early victim of the market slump and the uncertainty created by the action of United States Congress was the Churchill Falls stock issue. Shares put on the market by a Canadian-British group had to be withdrawn at the end of September. This was especially mortifying for the directors of the consortium who represent financial interests known the world over. Soon this setback was interpreted as a result of the "climate" existing in Quebec. In fact, it would have been a gamble in any event to sell shares that would bring no return for ten or fifteen years on a market made so nervous by the news from Washington and New York.

On October 3, the Premier of Quebec issued (from Hawaii) a statement in favour of federalism. This was interpreted in financial circles as a means of calming investors.

On October 6, the Toronto *Globe and Mail* ran a two-page spread on the flight of capital from Quebec. Transactions that had been in preparation for months were cited as evidence, along with some that had taken place long before. But no matter! The desired effect on public opinion called for taking a few liberties with chronology. . . .

The following day the *Financial Post,* also of Toronto, took up the story. At the same time, the President of the Montreal Stock Exchange made a smashing statement in the same vein. All these nice people obviously were acting out of great concern for "stability" in Quebec!

But the gaps between the bond yields remained the same. . . .

On October 14, the Quebec Liberal Party convention was held, leading to certain well-known resignations. In the days preceding it, Eric Kierans revived the theme of the flight of capital, and returned to the failure of the Churchill Falls stock issue as an example. . . .

In the wake of such manoeuvers, rumours ran riot and newspaper headlines and TV programs on the subject multiplied. A note of urgency crept into the paternal words of caution of certain "master thinkers."

October 13, amid pressure such as had not been seen for a long, long time, Quebec bonds finally slipped, and the gaps in yield rates increased. The yield on Quebec bonds rose to 0.8 per cent in relation to Ontario and 1.3 per cent in relation to Government of Canada bonds in the following days.

Finally, Marcel Faribault was named to the Legislative Council as economic and constitutional adviser to the Quebec government. The market interpreted this nomination as a proof that the government was "getting into line." Next day the President of the Montreal Stock Exchange announced that the flight of capital now would level off. . . .

The end of the story is obvious. A short time later the gaps between interest rates for Quebec, Ontario, and Ottawa savings bonds returned to normal.

Thus it was demonstrated to public opinion, all the more trusting because it was given so little information, that separatism is dangerous beyond a doubt and, above all, that the best governments are those ready to admit that financial circles still have some power to put the brakes on.

As a postscript to this episode, it is useful to note that after October (but not before) a great many savings bonds were sold in Quebec. Anoher proof of the flight of capital? We might also recall that a new issue of Canada Savings Bonds came out at this time, and that its interest rate was 5.5 per cent or the same as that of Quebec. The previous year the Quebec government, to fight similar competition, had raised its rate. In 1967, it did not do so. . . .*

*Note: This brief sketch, which shows only the part of the iceberg visible above the surface, is the result of a modest piece of teamwork. Some of our experts in search of subjects to explore would certainly find it a profitable study to complete. It might even be useful to the people of Quebec!

Conclusion

From Economics to Politics

The changes proposed herein—sovereignty, association, transition period, etc.—are not all that hard to swallow, *if.* . . .

If we really want to surmount the difficulties, and know how to go about it.

Which brings us back to politics, the area of the collective will. Here is where men make the decisions (or are afraid or neglect to make them) required for the smooth operation of their common interests.

For in the last analysis, however important our economic life may be, it depends greatly on the quality of the policies created and administered by the state for the benefit of everyone.

Economics may have its laws, but like other precepts gathered from experience most of them remain subject to the behaviour of that supreme variable known as man.

These laws can be usefully applied only if a people and its leaders, having understood them, follow them to the best of their ability in an intelligent and flexible manner, attuned to the perpetual changes in the "economic situation."

This means that in a field of study rich in complex recipes and in solutions that are both debatable and hotly disputed, there is after all only one absolute law of economics, and it is as essential as a compass in the forest: it is the law of clear-thinking responsibility.

This is of capital importance to a people on the eve of acquiring its liberty. The most important interpretation of that liberty, at the beginning and forever after, is in fact that a people accept full responsibility for its fate, just as an individual becomes responsible for his acts on coming of age.

Liberty, maturity, responsibility: three closely related notions —if not, in fact, completely equivalent.

The Impossibility of Non-Dependance

A sophisticated people cannot, therefore, with impunity neglect the most responsible and clear kind of thinking on the subject of its imminent liberation.

It will be forced immediately to see and admit that it must impose restraints upon itself, especially in the economic sphere.

We have already said this, or implied it, but it may be useful to repeat it in order to exercise completely certain devils in the form of pernicious delusions: there no longer is such a thing as a "non-dependent" country, not anywhere in the world; not even the United States, and when we have said that we have said everything.

The international society of nations has, in this connection, a kind of code of ethics, of the "Thou shalt" and the "Thou shalt not" variety, and its members are expected to learn the code and practise it if they want to be respected. It is remarkable that among the advanced countries even the most intractable in other fields usually obey with some scrupulousness these rules of economic etiquette.

To begin with, they obey those concerning their own internal equilibrium, establishing the limits within which excessive inflation can be avoided, as well as excessive deficits and the more easily visible illnesses such as devaluation. A country that cannot resist the diverse temptations that lead to these problems is taken to be irresponsible, and as all these infections are more or less contagious, the victim does himself as much harm abroad as at home. We need only think of the horrid headache that has afflicted everyone as a result of the ill-health into which the United Kingdom has been plunged these last few years, and the price the U.K. has paid—a price so exorbitant that de Gaulle has been blamed!

There are also many restraints imposed on any state by its membership in the vast club of international trade. We shall only mention, as examples, only the very strict rules with which its customs practices must comply if it wishes to belong to GATT; and the good resolutions it has to make in order to join the International Monetary Fund, the good advice it will have to take in case of an appeal, and even, when in need of help, the bitter pill it may have to swallow in having to open its books for examination and perhaps having to accept severe conditions.

And then there are those more special bonds which peoples create between each other, in pairs and in groups, in acknowledgement of their interdependence (as necessary as it is profitable). From these agreements there is a natural flow of other obligations which a signatory nation ignores only at the price of its reputation.

The economic association we propose, once the "contract" had been signed, would obviously involve obligations of this sort, which Quebec would have obliged to respect scrupulously. Thus, a treaty for a common market must prevent its members from favouring their own national products by means of tax relief or subsidies and thus re-erecting internally the tariff barriers the parties had agreed to abolish. In the same way, monetary union implies that if a particular monetary policy is adopted by the partners, Quebec should not introduce fiscal measures that contradict rather than support that policy.

But to pretend, as some have done, that this kind of restraint would be equivalent to fiscal servitude, or even that it would inevitably condemn Quebec to a return to federalism, is to ignore a very real difference in the two situations. Those who are unable to see the difference are victims of a rather unreasonable relapse into the worst kind of French-Canadian inferiority complex. They say, in effect, that Quebec is congenitally and incurably under-age, that responsible freedom is an impossibility for Quebec, and that it will never be able to live except under foreign tutelage!

The reasonable and mutually advantageous co-ordination demanded by any kind of economic association (with or without monetary union) in no way prevents two soveign states from remaining quite distinct territories from a fiscal standpoint. To maintain the contrary is to restrict us to a kind of delirious impotence . . . or afflict us with the blindspots that partisan attitudes sometimes induce in even the best minds.

"Masters in our Own House"

Even with all the necessary restraints established and accepted, a free people is no less free, and a sovereign state no less sovereign.

A sovereign Quebec takes back to its own house *in toto* all the powers and all the financial resources of the public sector.

It thus has in its own hands all the essential means of decision and the total product of its fiscal efforts.

Its remaining task is that of making *choices*—and this is the meaning of freedom.

It must choose its priorities, choose the direction its development should take, choose the groups and sectors that should be helped or stimulated in preference to others, *choose,* in fact, the kind of human society we want to become.

This liberty to choose the use we should make of our resources—and consequently the kind of society we prefer—is the only thing that really counts.

It is the indispensable chance that we as *Québécois* owe ourselves, following the example of so many other peoples, to build by and for ourselves the kind of country we want to have.

We believe in the necessity of seizing this enormous and challenging opportunity, for we are firmly convinced that this Quebec we build will be infinitely more efficient, prosperous, just, open to others, and sure of itself than the Quebec of today. And we believe that all these changes will never come about under the present regime.

Epilogue

*Minorities are good for nothing unless
they are ready to fight.*

Lawrence Durrell, *Mountolive*

QUEBEC

*Quebec is a growing word. It also is a territory. A place of
migrations. Of cold. Of snow. Where do you see as many birds?
And what rivers! Where are there as many waterways?—right
up to the endless ice! The darling of geographers and ornithologists.*

*But the danger of words that are used for geography is that
they also reach out to us. What is this anxiety that drives men
to seek refuge in a word? What have we to do with this word,
whose warmth seems more and more necessary to us in living
out what we have to live? And is it a good enough reason for
us to go against the grain of history?*

*The lowliest animal implacably defends his territory accord-
ing to his nature. Even the air is shared among the birds. We
are not dealing here with justice or with law but with biology.
The smallest nation stubbornly calls itself a kingdom. Do we
need to look farther for an explanation?*

*Words also increase the risk of error. All words are prophets,
in a small way. And is it unreasonable to hope? Perhaps we
need only choose our words carefully . . . so as to make them
possible among all the words that belong to history and
geography.*

*And yet they have left their mark in the flower of this
language on more lands than any other people and on more
rivers than in any other country. Is that enough to win them a
grant of some part of the kingdom? But words themselves cannot even agree. Who manipulates them after his own whim?
There is the word "Labrador" and the word "Minganie." There
is that "Ysle des ouaiseaulx" which Cartier named, and where
he made his first landfall. Who but the ornithologists knows that
it now bears the name of Funk Island?*

*On this arid rock where only storms can grow, a million
marmettes come each spring to lay and hatch their pear-shaped
eggs in the still-visible ruins of the great rookeries formerly oc-*

cupied by the big penguins described by Cartier which by now
are extinct:

"And there are in this place birds as large as geese, black
and white, with beaks like those of crows. . . . They have little
wings, like half a hand; with which they fly as strongly within
the water as other birds in the air. The said isle is as covered
with them as a meadow is with grass."

And they have no other kingdom but this rock and these
crannies in which they live their whole long lives. In the
same way men cannot leave their matrix of words. They
are lodged in perpetuity within the fragile membrane of
their mother tongue. There are poets who speak of a "word-
less land." Are they deaf? And what if our language is a
rock . . . an escarpment . . . a high cliff! And if I in my
turn have discovered all these shores, these rivers and islands,
without ever having been a traveller or a geographer, I had
no other clue but language—language explored to its re-
motest outposts.

Without this heritage, without this bird-covered rock, I
would not dare pronounce the word québec, for it is not a
word for playing make-believe.

And I would be like Etienne Bujold from Bonaventure,
who dared to take a chance in Montreal so as to live a
little better than his father had done . . . though he had
been taught that poverty would guarantee him a place in
heaven.

My father told me . . . my mother told me: "Don't you know
we're lucky to be poor?" I never understood that . . . how we
were lucky because we were poor. And I was poor in the sense
that I lacked the bare necessities.

The bread was there. Instead of taking it, I said, "It's because
the good Lord wills it that I'm poor." I wasn't poor. I was a
coward. But they had preached submissiveness to us.

If I didn't know them, if I hadn't listened to them until the
small hours, these men who live in a city owned by some
through the sweat of others, these men-who-are-good-for-
talking, I would not claim the rock of birds and I would feel
as Etienne felt when he came to Montreal from his native
countryside because life there was no longer possible for the
living.

I was used to having space around me. We had a little farm back there. We were at home.

What future is there for all of them? What kind of happiness in Montreal where they try to find a place for themselves, a balcony, a stairway, a Sunday, an alleyway, a courtyard, a little turret, an attic window, another Sunday, someone to love and a roostful of children . . .

These displaced country folk.

And here I was in the house of a stranger . . . working for a stranger, riding in a stranger's tramways; nothing belonged to me, it always belonged to strangers.

. . . and always to the same ones, needless to say . . .

I was never at home . . . and anyone could have said to me, "Why don't you go home?" but I didn't know where to go when they said, "Why don't you go home?"

We have all known it well, this feeling of displacement: the uninhabitable land. We were a people without a king, shifting like gypsies, and every year in May trying to find our homeland at the top of some stairway.

But we still had our acharnation—our "stubbornation," that staggering word invented by Alexis Tremblay from the Ile aux Coudres to describe our character. For Alexis, to have character was to be

"Like us, if you will. We're almost eighty . . . Our children stick by us. They cling to the family blood, first of all. And they want us around. . . . It's stubbornation I'm talking about."

We still had our stubbornation, our acharnation. Is not the earth carnal, like the language we drink with the milk of the first words? Man clings to this flesh of his flesh. He cannot prevent the consequences of his blood. And the best proof of the mother's blood is the language of her children. And the proof of a people's blood is the whole language, nourished by sea and land. . . .

But I will not tell here all my admiration for it.

A country is nothing but an experiment in pride. We shall not escape unscathed from this song, for we have committed the indiscretion of loving the land as a country.

Pierre Perrault